# Conflict, Education and People's War in Nepal

This book presents an overview of the democracy movement and the history of education in Nepal. It shows how schools became the battleground for the state and the Maoists as well as captures emerging trends in the field, challenges for the state and negotiations with political commitments. It looks at the factors that contributed to the conflict, and studies the politics of the region alongside gender and identity dynamics.

One of the first studies on the subject, the book highlights how conflict and education are intrinsically linked in Nepal. It illustrates how schools became the centre of attention between warring groups and how they were used for political meetings and recruitment of fighters during the political transitions in a contested terrain in South Asia. It brings to the fore incidents of abduction and killing of teachers and students, and the use of children as porters for arms and ammunitions. Drawing extensively on both primary and secondary sources and qualitative analyses, the book provides the key to a complex web of relationships among the stakeholders during conflict and also models of education in post-conflict situations.

This book will interest scholars and researchers in education, politics, peace and conflict studies, sociology, development studies, social work, strategic and security studies, contemporary history, international relations, and Nepal and South Asian studies.

**Sanjeev Rai** is Senior Education Specialist with the Swedish Committee for Afghanistan. Previously, he has worked with the Education Above All foundation (Qatar), Save the Children, UNICEF, CARE and the Aga Khan Foundation in India, as well as with media and academia. His expertise is in education in conflict situations, school and teacher education, and research and advocacy. He completed his MA in Political Science from the University of Allahabad and M. Ed., M.Phil. and Ph.D. in Education from the University of Delhi, India. With his experience in journalism, he writes for leading Indian publications and has authored many papers and reports. He is one of the key founder members of the Right to Education Forum, India, and has served as a steering group member of the Education Global Initiative of Save the Children International. He is the co-chair of the alliance on education in conflict and post-conflict countries established by the Global Education and Skills Forum, 2017.

# Nepal and Himalayan Studies

This series brings the larger Nepal and the Himalayan region to the centre stage of academic analysis and explores critical questions that confront the region, ranging from society, culture and politics to economy and ecology. The books in this series examine key themes concerning religion, ethnicity, language, identity, history, tradition, community, polity, democracy, as well as emerging issues regarding environment and development of this unique region.

**Nepali Diaspora in a Globalised Era**
*Edited by Tanka B. Subba and A. C. Sinha*

**Goddesses of Kathmandu Valley**
Grace, Rage, Knowledge
*Arun Gupto*

**The Himalayas and India–China Relations**
*Devendra Nath Panigrahi*

**Democratisation in the Himalayas**
Interests, Conflicts and Negotiations
*Edited by Vibha Arora and N. Jayaram*

**Sex Work in Nepal**
The Making and Unmaking of a Category
*Lisa Caviglia*

**State, Society and Health in Nepal**
*Madhusudan Subedi*

**Conflict, Education and People's War in Nepal**
*Sanjeev Rai*

For a full list of titles in this series, please visit www.routledge.com/Nepal-and-Himalayan-Studies/book-series/NHS

# Conflict, Education and People's War in Nepal

Sanjeev Rai

LONDON AND NEW YORK

First published 2018
by Routledge
2 Park Square, Milton Park, Abingdon, Oxon OX14 4RN

and by Routledge
711 Third Avenue, New York, NY 10017

*Routledge is an imprint of the Taylor & Francis Group, an informa business*

© 2018 Sanjeev Rai

The right of Sanjeev Rai to be identified as author of this work has been asserted by him in accordance with sections 77 and 78 of the Copyright, Designs and Patents Act 1988.

All rights reserved. No part of this book may be reprinted or reproduced or utilised in any form or by any electronic, mechanical, or other means, now known or hereafter invented, including photocopying and recording, or in any information storage or retrieval system, without permission in writing from the publishers.

*Trademark notice*: Product or corporate names may be trademarks or registered trademarks, and are used only for identification and explanation without intent to infringe.

*British Library Cataloguing-in-Publication Data*
A catalogue record for this book is available from the British Library

*Library of Congress Cataloging-in-Publication Data*
A catalog record for this book has been requested

ISBN: 978-1-138-69138-4 (hbk)
ISBN: 978-1-351-06674-7 (ebk)

Typeset in Sabon
by Apex CoVantage, LLC

*Amma-Papa ji,* and my beloved niece, Shambhavi.
(I wish they could have stayed longer with us!)

# Contents

| | | |
|---|---|---|
| *List of figures* | | viii |
| *Foreword* | | ix |
| *Acknowledgements* | | xi |
| 1 | Conflict and education: the relationship | 1 |
| 2 | Emergence of Nepal and movements for democracy | 24 |
| 3 | State and education provisions in the backdrop of the People's War | 45 |
| 4 | Schools: the battleground | 64 |
| 5 | Post-People's War: complexity and hope | 98 |
| | *Annexure I: letter to revise curriculum and content* | 110 |
| | *Annexure II: countries affected with conflict* | 114 |
| | *References* | 116 |
| | *Appendix* | 129 |
| | *Index* | 133 |

# Figures

| | | |
|---|---|---|
| 1.1 | Galtung's models of conflict, violence and peace | 2 |
| 1.2 | Conflict escalation and de-escalation | 4 |
| 1.3 | The hourglass model: conflict containment, conflict settlement and conflict transformation | 7 |
| 4.1 | Acknowledging contribution of the community in constructing a school building | 68 |
| 4.2 | Photograph of King Gyanendra and his family members in an old textbook | 72 |

# Foreword

Social strife and political conflict affect the lives of not merely those who are directly engaged in them, but large segments of bystanders, those who live and work in such zones, who become unwittingly part of the 'collateral damage' (an anaesthetised and dehumanised jargon that stubbornly refuses to acknowledge the intensity of such human experiences). Their lives are disrupted irreparably because they are at the wrong place at the wrong time. Some are killed in crossfire, many are maimed, and many more lose their homes and livelihoods. Some are forcibly made participants in the conflict. It is always the poor, the weak and the vulnerable that are the most affected. Children are particularly vulnerable. For children, the loss is irreparable, irretrievable, for they lose their childhoods and opportunities for learning and growing. This has been the sad story in every conflict situation across the continents – in Colombia, in Rwanda, in Afghanistan, in Syria and in several conflict zones in South Asia.

Nepal witnessed a period of intense political conflict during the 1990s and the first decade of the present century in the form of insurgency led by the Maoists, in the ambience of a simmering popular dissatisfaction about the continuance of the monarchy and mass aspirations for democracy. Normal life remained disrupted in many parts of the country for long periods of time. One institution that was most affected was school. School was the major focal point in the conflict – both physical and ideological. On the one hand, most school buildings in the conflict zones were occupied by either the insurgents or the government troops, and on the other, school curriculum became a contested territory where the Maoists sought to bring about drastic changes in substance and methodology. Needless to say, the children and the teachers were the most affected by this difficult situation, which stretched on for years.

Documentation of how conflict impacts education has been in short supply. There has been very little by way of systematic study and theorisation. In this context, the present book by Sanjeev Rai assumes immense significance. It is based on extensive fieldwork and testimonies of a large number of people – the protagonists in the conflict, those who have suffered as part of the 'collateral damage' and those who have observed the conflict from the periphery.

This book explores the underlying sociopolitical structures, relationships and historical factors that define the complex terrain and render education as a contested territory in situations of conflict. This exploration is of immense relevance, as new dimensions of conflict unfold globally every time in one zone of political unrest or the other, and education becomes a casualty in most such situations, with more and more schools and institutions of higher learning coming under siege directly or indirectly. The attempt in this book is to capture some of the most significant trends as regards education and conflict, drawing parallels between what happened in Nepal in those years of Maoist insurgency and some of the recent occurrences of intense strife in theatres of conflict that range from Syria to Pakistan. The book also attempts to analyse the dynamics of the difficult relationship between conflict and education and examine them and the larger societal context in which they act out, in a coherent perspective. This is doubtless the essential first step towards the much needed building of theories that would help serious scholars to make sense of the complex dynamics of conflict and education.

Authenticity, rigor and attempt to present complexities with coherence are the major strengths of this book. It is rendered in a style that makes it accessible to scholars and students both of education and politics, as well as to general readers with curiosity about contemporary social and political developments.

**Shyam B. Menon**
Vice Chancellor, Ambedkar University Delhi (AUD),
New Delhi, India

# Acknowledgements

This book has evolved progressively up to the current shape with the support of numerous people.

First and foremost, my teacher, Professor Shyam B. Menon, Vice Chancellor of AUD, India: a special thanks to him for his consistent guidance and insightful discussions, and for always showing me the broader canvas of life.

I would extend my sincere gratitude to Shri Ram Bahadur Rai, senior journalist and Chairperson, Indira Gandhi National Centre for the Arts (IGNCA), and Shri Anand Swaroop Verma, senior journalist, who gave me relevant contacts to get a deeper understanding of the issue.

I owe a special debt of gratitude to Dr Geeta Menon, Professor Srinivas Rao, Desmond Bermingham, Indivar Mukhopadhyey and Satya Narayan Mishra Sir for their encouragement to have the book published.

In addition, I am thankful to several friends and scholars for their constructive comments and suggestions on the draft of various chapters. The list of dedicated reviewers includes Randeep Kaur, Anu Singh Chaudhary, Ambrish Rai, Kopal Chaube, Harshvardhan Kumar, Angana and Swati Mohan.

This work is the result of continued inspiration and motivation given by my wife, Alka. She stands beside me throughout my career and writing this book. She is the pillar of my strength. My wonderful son and daughter, Bihu and Kuhu, were ten and one at the time of writing this book. They always make me smile. They had to show patience when their father was working on this book, instead of taking them out on weekends.

I am thankful to Punam Thankur for her valuable inputs and editorial support at the early stage of the manuscript. My sincere thanks to Aakash Chakrabarty and Avneet Kaur of Routledge for their hard work and cooperation. I really enjoyed working with the Routledge team.

Last, but definitely not the least, I am grateful to the children, officials, teachers, academia, journalists and common people of Nepal for their kind-heartedness. Without their extended support, I could have not gained the courage and knowledge to work on this book.

# 1 Conflict and education
## The relationship

### Understanding conflict

Images of the children and teachers killed on 16 December 2014 in a military school in Peshawar in Pakistan are still fresh in public memory. This was the first of its kind of attack in which more than 141 children and six school personnel were murdered in their own school; 113 people including children were injured in the attack (DAWN, 2004). The horrific incident also marked a shift from merely attacking school buildings to killing innocent children in their school premises.

Of course, Peshawar was not the only incident in which innocent school children were targeted. Aerial bombings of schools have also been observed in Gaza and Syria in the recent past. Given this situation, it does not come as a surprise that the number of out-of-school children in conflict zones is more than 28.5 million, and globally more than 57 million children are out of school (UNESCO, 2013). This comes at a time when the world is witnessing an increase in armed conflicts, and the very nature of their occurrence is also changing.

The quickly changing nature of conflict requires a new lens to understand the newer complexities, as traditional norms are no longer relevant in conflicts. Further, the line between lawful and unlawful actors, states and non-state actors, police and civilians is getting blurred (Kaldor & Luckham, 2001).

*Academic attention*

Conflict has received worldwide attention from researchers and academics who explain their own interpretations of violence and conflict. The word 'conflict' derives from the Latin word *confligere*, which means literally to 'strike together'. Within the human realm, conflict occurs when different social groups are rivals or otherwise in

## 2  Conflict and education: the relationship

competition. Such conflicts may have different outcomes for the people involved in a conflict and for those affected by it – some may die while others may change dramatically.

Peace researcher Quincy Wright identifies four factors which contribute in a conflict: idealistic, psychological, political and legal.

Researchers give other reasons why individuals and people have been moved to war. These are because they believe in the ideals that are expressed in symbols of religion, an empire, a nation or a civilisation and because they want to escape the situation that they are in and are hopeful that war will in some way lead to a betterment of their situation.

Further, government and factional groups have their own reasons for starting wars. These include war being a convenient way for them to carry out a foreign policy or to establish, maintain or expand their powers and because they feel that certain events that have occurred have violated law and violated their rights, and hence there is no choice for them but to wage a war.

The conflict analysis model proposed by Galtung in 1969 includes both symmetric and asymmetric conflicts. Galtung suggests that conflict could be viewed as a triangle, with contradiction (C), attitude (A) and behaviour (B) at its vertices (see Figure 1.1). Here the contradiction refers to the underlying conflict situation, which includes the actual or perceived 'incompatibility of goals' between the conflict parties generated by what Chris Mitchell calls a 'mis-match between social values and social structure' (1981, p. 18).

In a symmetric conflict, the contradiction is defined by the parties, their interests and the clash of interests between them.

In an asymmetric conflict, the contradiction is defined by the parties, their relationship and the conflict of interests inherent in the relationship.

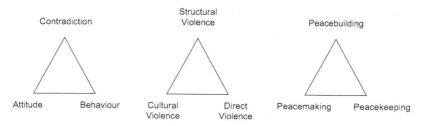

*Figure 1.1* Galtung's models of conflict, violence and peace

Source: Johan Galtung, *Violence, War, and Their Impact on Visible and Invisible Effects of Violence*, https://them.polylog.org/5/fgj-en.htm#s1

While attitude includes the parties' perceptions and misperceptions of each other and of themselves, these can be positive or negative. However, in violent conflicts, parties tend to develop demeaning stereotypes of the other, and attitudes are often influenced by emotions such as fear, anger, bitterness and hatred. Attitude also covers emotive (feeling), cognitive (belief) and conative (desire, will) elements. Analysts who emphasise these subjective aspects are said to have an expressive view of the sources of conflict. For example, Kriesberg (1982, p. 17) points out 'a social conflict exists when two or more parties believe they have incompatible objectives'.

Behaviour is the third component of the triangle. It can involve cooperation or coercion, gestures signifying conciliation or hostility. Violent conflict behaviour is characterised by threats, coercion and destructive attacks. Analysts who emphasise objective aspects such as structural relationships and competing material interests or behaviour are said to have an instrumental view of the sources of conflict (for example, there is conflict 'whenever incompatible actions occur . . . an action that is incompatible with another action prevents, obstructs, interferes, injures or in some way makes the latter less likely to be effective', Deutsch, 1973, p. 10).

Galtung sees conflict as a dynamic process in which structure, attitudes and behaviour are constantly changing and influencing one another. As the dynamic develops, it becomes a manifest conflict formation, as parties' interests clash or the relationship they are in becomes oppressive. Parties then organise around this structure to pursue their interests. They develop hostile attitudes and conflictual behaviour. And so the conflict formation starts to grow and intensify.

He indicates two roots: a culture of violence (heroic, patriotic, patriarchal, etc.) and a structure that itself is violent by being too repressive, exploitative or alienating, too tight or too loose for the comfort of people (Galtung, 1998).

The visible effects of direct violence are known: the killed, the wounded, the displaced, the material damage, all increasingly hitting civilians. But the invisible effects may be even more vicious: direct violence reinforces structural and cultural violence. The most important aspect, however, is hatred and the addiction to revenge for the trauma suffered among the losers, and to more victories and glory among the winners.

In the course of a conflict, it can also happen that it may widen, drawing in other parties, and deepen and spread, generating secondary conflicts within the main parties or among outsiders who get sucked in. This often complicates the task of addressing the original, core conflict considerably.

## 4  Conflict and education: the relationship

Eventually, however, resolving the conflict must involve a set of dynamic changes. A related idea due to Galtung (1990) is the distinction between direct violence (children are murdered), structural violence (children die through poverty) and cultural violence (whatever blinds us to this or seeks to justify it). We end direct violence by changing conflict behaviour, structural violence by removing structural contradictions and injustices, and cultural violence by changing attitudes.

## Conflict escalation and de-escalation

New issues and conflict parties can emerge, internal power struggles can alter tactics and goals and secondary conflicts and spirals can further complicate the situation. The same is true of de-escalation, with unexpected breakthroughs and setbacks changing the dynamics, with advances in one area or at one level being offset by relapses in others and with the actions of third parties influencing the outcome in unforeseen ways. Figure 1.2 shows a simplified model in which escalation phases move along a normal distribution curve from the initial differences that are a part of all social developments, through the emergence of an original contradiction that may or may not remain latent, to the process of polarisation in which antagonistic parties form and the conflict becomes manifest and culminates in the outbreak of direct violence and war (Glasl, 1982; Fisher & Keashly, 1991) (Figure 1.2).

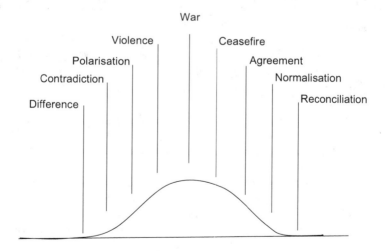

*Figure 1.2* Conflict escalation and de-escalation

Source: Chapter 1, Introduction to Conflict Resolution: Concepts and Definitions, www.polity.co.uk/ccr/contents/chapters/RAMSBOTHAMCh01.pdf

Social constructivists consider material and communicative power as a fundamental way of understanding conflicts and related incidents (Conteh-Morgan, 2004, p. 18). The role of norms, ideas, identity and group constructs are significant factors for constructivists. The circumstances shape the norms which define reality in a given context, so that it can be changed over time. Constructivists believe that social belief and identity are the result of group association and the environment that they live in. Identity issue is one of the dominant factors resulting in conflicts and depends on the collective understanding of inequalities, injustice, etc. (Hangen, 2010). Examples of this can be seen in some of the recent conflicts like the Tamil-Singhalese fight in Sri Lanka and the Hutu-Tutsi conflict in Rwanda.

Social constructivism believes that reality and knowledge are emergent and situated in the social environment and constructed as people engage with others in shared activities (New & Cochran, 2007, p. 744). This approach gives a perspective for understanding how group identities are formed. If a group feels threatened by any other group or by the state, group members try to achieve their common goal by any means. The culture of the group and the given contexts are the two important factors that help to construct knowledge, as members of society develop their own contextual meaning while interacting with community members. For constructivists, social processes are of much significance, as the notions of reality and knowledge depend on these processes. In the context of Sri Lanka's three decades of civil war, collective feelings of discrimination of the Tamil people helped them to form a strong group identity and they tried to attain their objectives by any means, including war with the state.

The theory of relative deprivation considers that long-pending grievances of social and economic development will lead to a revolution triggered by instant economic crisis. Davies (cited in Conteh-Morgan, 2004, p. 70) argues that revolution is the result of wide unbearable gaps between expectations and gratification in society.

In any society if economic gaps between the 'masses' and the 'classes' become broad, and marginalised people start realising fears of losing their possessed means, then tension among the groups could result in collective violence. Davies (cited in Conteh-Morgan, 2004, p. 70) explains his theoretical perspective with reference to many revolutions (the Russian revolution of 1917, American Civil War, etc.) across the world.

The relative deprivation approach considers economic deprivation and the state's failure to fulfil the expectations of the people as the reasons behind collective violence. During the transformation, it is crucial to maintain equilibrium between individuals' genuine needs and society's own capability to gratify them. Dichotomy in needs and capability shows the way for social instability. Gurr (cited in Conteh-Morgan, 2004, pp. 70–71) considers both psychological and societal variables to clarify causes of violence. He further explains the theory of relative deprivation in terms of a discrepancy between expectations and capabilities. If the gap between them is large, it could result in collective political violence in any society. Recent developments in South Sudan can be understood using this lens, as expectations from the government are very high but the capabilities of the government are limited, resulting in people's anger against the leaders.

In some groups, experiencing a sense of inequality appears to be a prime factor in enhancing tensions between groups or between groups and the state. Sears (2008) argues that inequalities in any society lead to a situation of conflict and actors question existing relations in the society to produce new structures and relationships through basic transformations. The state claims to serve all citizens, but actually supports and protects the interests of powerful groups. Therefore, disadvantaged people wish to play the role of change agents initially through legal channels, and if they do not find these existing ways effective, they may take up illegal routes to challenge the authority of the state. In the process of bringing a balance, the state may offer some symbolic representation to marginalised people in the power circuit (Sears, 2008).

The nature of warfare has changed today. Intra-state (war within states) conflict has replaced inter-state conflict (war between states) and new actors have become involved with new forms of organised violence. These increased complexities demand new sets of classifications and relationships to describe conflict. Different groups, such as ideological networks, ethnic groups, groups aligned on identity issues and political groups with armed wings, are actively contributing to the intra-state conflicts (Kaldor, 2006).

Conflicts can be resolved in many ways: by violence, by changes in issues over a period of time or by mutual agreement (Barash & Webel, 2002, p. 26).

The hourglass model represents the narrowing of political space that characterises conflict escalation, and the widening of political space that characterises conflict de-escalation. As the space narrows and widens, different conflict resolution responses become more or less appropriate or possible. This is a contingency and complementarity model, in which 'contingency' refers to the nature and phase of the conflict, and 'complementarity' to the combination of appropriate

Conflict and education: the relationship 7

responses that need to be worked together to maximise chances of success in conflict resolution (see Figure 1.3). This model distinguishes between the elite peacemaking that forms the substance of conflict settlement, and the deeper levels of peacemaking (including reconciliation) that are better seen as a part of cultural peacebuilding.

Conflict transformation is seen to encompass the deepest levels of cultural and structural peacebuilding. Conflict settlement (which many critics wrongly identify with conflict resolution) corresponds to what we call 'elite peacemaking' – in other words, negotiations or mediations among the main protagonists with a view to reaching a mutually acceptable agreement. Conflict containment includes preventive peacekeeping, war limitation and post-ceasefire peacekeeping. War

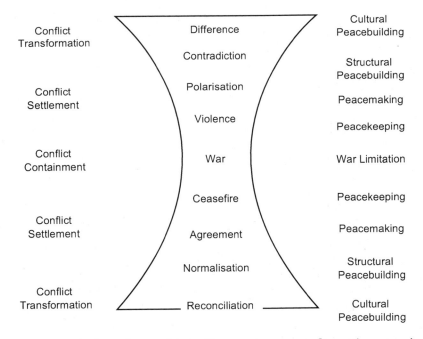

*Figure 1.3* The hourglass model: conflict containment, conflict settlement and conflict transformation

Note: In de-escalation phases conflict resolution tasks must be initiated at the same time and are nested. They cannot be undertaken sequentially as may be possible in escalation phases – see chapters 5 and 8. We suggest that what is sometimes called deep peacemaking (which includes reconciliation) is best seen as part of cultural peacebuilding.

Source: Ramsbotham, Miall & Woodhouse (2011). *Contemporary conflict resolution*

limitation includes attempts to constrain the fighting geographically, to mitigate and alleviate its intensity and to bring about its termination at the earliest possible moment.

## Understanding conflict from the education perspective

The relationship of education with conflict is a comparatively new perspective, as most of the conflict analysis frameworks consider factors like economy, ethnicity, governance and the distribution of natural resources to be more significant than education in states affected by conflict.

However, the figures for the relationship between education and conflict highlight the significance of understanding this relationship. For example, estimates say that currently 28 million children are out of school in countries affected by conflict (UNESCO, 2011, p. 132). In the last two decades the nature of conflict has changed, and children, teachers and schools have emerged as prime victims of violence within some countries.

The Global Coalition to Protect Education from Attack (GCPEA, 2014) documents attacks on schools and universities. In its 2014 report it estimated that 9,600 schools in 70 countries had been damaged, destroyed or occupied between 2009 and 2013. Afghanistan, Colombia, Pakistan, Somalia, Sudan and Syria are countries of major concern.

Like a war between nations, conflict within a country may have a political agenda of change rather than retaliation against a group or state forces. Countries like Afghanistan, Colombia, Sudan, Syria, the Democratic Republic of Congo, Pakistan, Iraq, Kenya, Libya, Egypt and Ethiopia have experienced frequent attacks on educational institutions and personnel during recent years. More than 40 countries, including France and the United Kingdom (GCPEA, 2014), have faced isolated attacks. In South Asia, with the exception of Bhutan, schools have been attacked in every country in recent years. The assumption of having greater peace after the end of the Cold War has not become reality. As Charles Tilly (2002, pp. 56–57) rightly observed, 'The number of civil wars expanded much more rapidly than the number of independent states, which rose from about 100 in 1960 to 161 in 1999.'

Ninety per cent of the targets of intra-state conflicts are civilians and schools, which have thus emerged as a strategic space for warring parties. Further, in addition to attacks on school buildings, children and teachers are being killed by both of the parties involved in armed conflicts. Says Kaldor, 'The present days conflict is more complex and appears as a mixture of war, organised crime and massive violations of human rights.'

Armed violence is the fourth leading cause of death worldwide for persons between the ages of 15 and 44 years. In more than 40 countries, it is one of the top 10 causes of death. In Latin America and Africa, armed violence is the seventh and ninth leading cause of death, respectively (SAS, Global Burden of Armed Violence, 2015). However, in the absence of data-tracking mechanisms and deeper research studies, very often violence-related issues have not been noticed and have not been included in public debates.

However, emerging trends show that some countries face more challenges from internal conflicts than from wars with neighbouring countries, and a few states spend more money on their internal security than they do on education. Afghanistan, Syria, South Sudan, Pakistan and Yemen are struggling with internal conflicts, and countries like China and India spend more money on their internal security than on education.

The changed nature of conflict and advanced technologies in arms and ammunitions have blurred the distinction between war zones and civil habitations. Technological advancements and easy access to arms have made possible gun battles between professionally trained state-armed forces and self-trained armed groups. Escalated armed conflicts compel states to divert resources from social welfare to military expenditure, adding more challenges for marginalised groups. Kaldor says,

> The new wars involve a blurring of the distinction between war (usually defined as violence between state or organised political groups for political motives), organised crime (violence undertaken by privately organised groups for private purposes, usually financial gain) and large-scale violations of human rights (violence undertaken by states or politically organised groups against individuals).
> (Blin, 2011, pp. 289–90)

Traditionally, education is seen as an investment for 'future citizens' but with growing internal violence and rapid emergence of armed groups within countries, scholars are keen to analyse the role of education in the context of conflict. The positive aspects of education – as a means of social/individual benefit and ensuring peace and promotion of values of coexistence – cannot be denied, but knowing how education contributes in spreading hatred towards others and leads to conflict also seem equally vital aspects.

The relationship between education and conflict is complex. Increasing attacks on schools, children and teachers cannot be considered merely as collateral damage of a fight between warring groups. The gravity of the situation can be gauged from the fact that between 2009 and 2012 armed groups, state military and other criminal groups targeted thousands of school children, university students, teachers, academics and education establishments in at least 70 countries worldwide (GCPEA, 2014). Even a casual glance of this data compels a need for deeper engagements with the issue.

The number of indirect deaths is often ignored, and a large number of people who are permanently physically disabled, as well as those with mental disabilities that are a consequence of conflict, do not appear in data. The Global Burden of Armed Violence report (2015) of Small Arms Survey estimates that

> at least 200,000 people – and perhaps many thousands more – have died each year in conflict zones from non-violent causes (such as malnutrition, dysentery, or other easily preventable diseases) that resulted from the effects of war on populations between 2004 and 2007, at least 208,300 violent deaths were recorded in armed conflicts – an average of 52,000 people killed per year. This is a conservative estimate including only *recorded* deaths: the real total may be much higher.

Education is no longer a privilege but a right in the 21st century, and with the growing influence of the human rights approach to education, it is only appropriate that it be viewed as a fundamental right of every child in every country. The onus to ensure this right lies in the hands of the leaders. In recent years, initiatives like the United Nations' Education for All and the Millennium Development Goals (MDGs) with budgetary commitments from respective governments have also contributed to the expansion of educational services to include marginalised children, but the attacks, bombings, kidnappings, torture and murder of students and teachers in school premises have become a serious challenge. As reported by the GCPEA in its 2014 report 'Education Under Attack', educational institutions and teachers, and students in Afghanistan, Colombia, Pakistan, Somalia, Sudan and Syria were attacked more frequently from 2009 to 2013. In Pakistan alone, in Taliban attacks on more than 800 schools, school buildings were burnt, almost 100 students and teachers were injured and 30 students and 20 teachers lost their lives. Similarly, in Colombia, 140 teachers were killed between 2009 and 2012 and 1,086 teachers received death threats in the same period.

The Global Burden of Armed Violence report of 2015 also captures an interesting analysis:

> Conflict-related deaths, which appear to have increased since 2005, are highly concentrated: three-quarters of all reported direct conflict deaths took place in just ten countries. Ending the armed conflicts in Afghanistan, Iraq, Pakistan, Somalia, and Sri Lanka in 2007 would have reduced the total number of direct conflict deaths by more than two-thirds.

It is not surprising that the poor state of education and denial of quality schooling may have contributed to escalating violence, as education indicators are not impressive in many of these countries.

In Rwanda, ethnic conflict between Hutu (the majority ethnic group) and Tutsi resulted in the killing of 800,000 people in 1994. It has been reported that classroom practices contributed to fuelling tensions while portraying one ethnic identity as the natural owner of the resources over others. Misinterpretation of historical facts made the two communities enemies instead of making them learn the value of coexistence (Flood, 2014).

When the conflict occurred in 1994, teachers became the target on ethnic lines and almost 75 per cent of the teachers in Rwanda were either killed or fled during the genocide, and 45 per cent of the schools were destroyed (Moshman, 2015; Roberts, 2005). Similarly, 95 per cent of the school buildings needed to be repaired in Timor-Leste after violence took place in the country in 2000 (Human Right, 2012).

Why are schools becoming targets of protests, ethnic clashes or conflicts between state and non-state actors? A deeper understanding of the complexity and discourse on conflict seems an urgent prerequisite for working not only with the communities and countries suffering currently but also for suggesting changes in the systems and processes so that risks of potential violence can be minimised in other countries.

## Children and armed conflict

In the past few decades, intra-state conflicts have affected the lives and protection of children in conflict-affected areas, and schools are no longer zones of peace. Conflict increases threats to children and violates the mandate for their protection provided by the United Nations Conventions on the Rights of the Child. At the same time, children became more vulnerable and easy targets for forced recruitments for armed conflicts. Exposure to violence and the challenges of survival also have adverse effects on the psychosocial well-being of children.

The importance of education is often undermined by all the parties involved in a conflict, as schools are converted into relief camps and are used for storing arms and ammunition, and as they become camps for militants and armed forces and recruitment centres and places for organising political rallies. All these different uses also mean that children stay out of school.

With the increasing number of cases of conflict, schools have emerged as strategic places for warring groups. Schools are being used for different purposes, from holding rallies to recruitment and storage, and so armed groups bombard and attack schools as they perceive them to be a manifestation of the state. On the other hand, state armed forces destroy school buildings so that armed groups cannot use them for shelter and storage. In Iraq, between March 2003 and October 2008, 31,598 attacks were recorded on educational institutions, and in Afghanistan between 2007 and 2008 the number of attacks on schools increased from 242 to 670 (Human Security Report, 2012).

The increase in internal social and political conflicts and the need to address their basic causes in order to prevent and resolve them through the education system have emerged as critical steps in today's world. Descriptive details of any conflict-ridden society can be found easily, but a bigger challenge is tracing the root causes and explaining the reasons for their occurrence in a particular society.

Along with the peace process, most of the conflict-ridden countries face challenges in restructuring their education systems to ensure peace dividends to children and teachers. In cases where the duration of the conflict goes beyond a decade, an entire generation grows up in a state of exile and perhaps with an unwillingness to return. Among the countries that have suffered from conflict, only a few have reworked their education strategies, whereas most of them engaged with ideas like rewriting history, changing their language policy and medium of instruction, introducing a new curriculum, developing textbooks and introducing peace education. While moving forward, leaders must work towards making education for peace and ensuring peace for education.

## Engaging with the theoretical framework: education and conflict

### The Marxist perspective

Ideologies are a significant component of individual and collective world views, and as such they can lead to perceptions that contribute to war making. Ideologies can be organised around religious traditions, or around secular ways of life, such as capitalism, Marxism-Leninism, democracy, aristocracy, conservatism, liberalism, ethnocentrism and nationalism. They can be powerful engines of human behaviour, but when ideologies come in conflict, they can contribute to war; because they are deeply held, significant perceived ideological differences can contribute to wars of extraordinary brutality, with little or no quarter asked or given.

According to orthodox Marxism (or Marxism-Leninism), capitalism results in two antagonistic classes – the proletariats (workers) and the bourgeoisie (owners), with the bourgeoisie (or the ruling class that owns the means of production) controlling the government machinery. War is an external manifestation of this class struggle. Therefore, wars will come to an end only when communism has triumphed worldwide, following a possibly quite violent 'transition' period from capitalism to socialism, a period known as 'the dictatorship of the proletariat'.

On the other hand, mainstream Western capitalist ideology, by contrast, implies that the potential of individual 'success' and social 'security' is greatest in a situation of maximum economic freedom for markets and of freedom of thought and of speech for individuals. Wars are caused by many factors, but most notably by perceived threats to human freedom, such as those allegedly posed by 'communist-inspired' revolutionary social and political movements (Barash & Webel, 2009).

The Marxist approach advocates radical changes in society and argues that revolution is a normal process as 'they resolve the basic contradictions that are built into the social arrangements' (Conteh-Morgan, 2005, p. 10). Marxist thinkers believe that society is divided into conflicting classes broadly composed of the haves and the have-nots. The class that owns and controls resources economically exploits the class that does not. The economic exploitation is compounded by social and cultural exclusion that is a consequence of social stratification. Althusser (cited in Apple, 1982, p. 92) argues that education is an apparatus for the state's ideology and public schooling is a form of ideological control imposed by the ruling class. The only way to break this cycle of exploitation and exclusion in the Marxist perspective is revolution, which would lead to a social structure based on equality and social justice. In many countries, such as Nepal, India Maoists are the party of the conflict and their ideology has been derived from the Marxist perspective as they perceive that revolution is the only solution for ensuring social equity in society.

The smooth functioning of formal schools in a society has always been perceived as an indicator of normalcy, but Marxist scholars are of the opinion that state-controlled education is a mechanism to perpetuate the division between the masses and classes, leading to the reproduction of a social class. In contrast, what has also been observed and experienced is that whatever the degree of state control on education, the existing system prepares some people to play a catalyst's role in society. State actors often neglect and suppress the demand created by the catalysts and also by the leaders of marginalised groups to change the existing system to accommodate a wider group. Demand for change by the majority is constantly being raised and simultaneously numerous attempts are made to maintain status quo through policies and the police. If a situation like this prevails for a long period, and the masses feel neglected, conflict cannot be avoided, as it happened in Nepal. UNICEF's State of the World's Children Report (2005b) rightly predicted that if conflict continues in more than 70 countries, 75 million children will not be in primary schools by 2015 making the second Millennium Development Goal of achieving universal primary education unrealistic.

In contrast to the Marxist approach, the functionalist perspective emphasises why societies continue in spite of unending conflicts. Talcott Parsons (cited in Conteh-Morgan, 2005, p. 11) sees society as governed by self-correcting processes that serve to maintain an equilibrium. Functionalists consider society as an organism and good working order as essential for its smooth functioning and stability. A system is generally considered open, or designed to receive inputs from its environment. The system in turn influences environmental conditions to maintain its own stability. In particular, the functional prerequisites must be satisfied if a system is to survive or remain in an adequate working order.

Leading functionalists, such as Talcott Parsons and Chalmers Johnson specify four prerequisites. First is socialisation or pattern maintenance, which corresponds to the religious sectors of social life and involves, in particular, the inculcation of societal values and norms in children. Second, adapting to the environment underscores the political sectors of society related to the differentiation and allocation of roles, as well as the distribution of scarce resources. Third, attaining goals focuses on economic sectors of social life and is concerned with the formation and development of policies for achieving systemic goals. Fourth is integration and social control, which are preoccupied with the legal sectors of social life, justice, law and order, or ways in which problems of deviancy are prevented or solved (Conteh-Morgan, 2005).

A social system works like an input-output process model. Environmental conditions get treated as feedback and determine whether the system needs to change in order to maintain stability. If the system fails to respond adequately and promptly, it may be an indication that the environmental conditions are precipitating a revolution. These circumstances could challenge the predominant values and systems that are in place and in response ruling elites will either allow structural changes in the system or try to maintain the system through oppressive means. The nature of the structural change depends on who leads the agenda. Change will be conservative if it is being initiated by the elites. Revolutionary change occurs if the masses experience unfairness in distribution of justice for a long time.

## Schooling and conflict

Often, existing social orders are maintained through inculcation of faith among young children. The state also uses this mechanism for securing its authority primarily through revenues and state-controlled curricula, the national anthem, a language policy and through textbooks. This may probably be one of the reasons why educational opportunities were limited only to children of privileged people in many countries for a very long time. The masses who formed the base of the social pyramid had neither access to educational opportunities for their children nor did they have any stake in the processes. This situation changed in the later part of the 1990s and schooling was ensured for a majority of children across the world after the Jomtian conference and commitments by the governments on Education for All.

Right to Education is being advocated by civil society groups in developing and underdeveloped countries, and an in-principle commitment has been made by most of the nations for providing this, but emerging conflicts place a new challenge before children and parents. Conflicts render children more vulnerable and totally robbed of a normal life and routine. They are forced onto the streets, or to work as sex slaves, porters or perhaps even join armed groups. Beverly Roberts (2005) explains the case of out-of-school children in North Uganda who became sex slaves, resulting in many girls becoming teenage mothers. Needless to say, the girls who are trapped in this cycle are in the worst situation. Malala Yousafzai in the Swat District of Pakistan's north-western Khyber Pakhtunkhwa province is an exceptional case. She survived after an attack by Tehreek-e-Taliban in 2012 and has now become a global icon.

At another level, a majority of the girls who are in armed groups are often invisible and face sexual violence. Soldiers, enemies and even their own group leaders exploit them. A majority of the girls join armed groups out of compulsion, while some opt for joining armed groups for security and livelihood reasons, as they cannot expect better jobs because of the poor education of only a few years in their normal lives (McKay & Mazurana, 2004). When these girls want to return to their communities, ensuring their acceptance in their families and communities is not an easy task.

Conflict also has a direct relationship with the economic situation of a country, as most of the countries caught in conflict are of middle and low income populations. Governments add to the challenges of prioritising education over other sectors as a result of weak political will. A majority of the government schools normally do not appear as centres of excellence and provide lower quality education. Lack of a common school system means that children of well-to-do families study in private schools or in limited exclusive government schools meant for the children of military officials and government administrators. These two parallel school systems not only create a wide gap in education attainment but also lead to better income and positioning of the privileged group. This may be one of the reasons that parents, particularly those who cannot afford private schools, keep their children out of school in a situation of perceived threat, as they do not see the forward linkages of schooling available for their wards. This sense of educational marginalisation helps political and armed groups to mobilise against the state and the privileged groups.

Public schooling is also seen as an essential mechanism of integration (Tawil, 2004). Most of the socially excluded communities have found the roots of exclusion within the school system in their respective societies. Bernal (1977) endorses this line of thinking and recognises that marginalisation, social inequity and exclusion fomented by schools deprived many Colombian citizens of a chance to legally participate in society. If a group of people experience discrimination by public and legal institutions for a long period, they may adopt illegal ways and violent acts in reaction (Davies, 2004).

Even in cases where children continue to access schools, they do so in an atmosphere of uncertainty. Article 28(A) of the UN Convention on the Rights of the Child states: 'Make primary education compulsory and available and free to all' (United Nations, 1989). However, it is not a coincidence that more than half of the out-of-school children live in countries touched by conflict. For instance, in Palestine alone more than one lakh children in the primary age group do not have access to schools. Her Majesty Queen Rania Al Abdullah of Jordan rightly pointed out, 'Growing up in the shadow of occupation, scarred by conflict, going to school remains the single most cherished priority of Palestinian children. Despite bombs and blockades, they know it's their only hope for a normal life' (UNESCO, 2011).

## School, child soldiers and light-weight weapons

Advancements in technologies are fast emerging as a double-edged sword. On the one hand, advancement in information and communication technologies is being used to improve educational attainments on a pilot basis in many countries, but the technological advancements in arms and ammunition have resulted in light-weight, more sophisticated weapons, which have changed the nature of conflict and the roles of civilians and children in these conflicts. Experience shows that earlier fewer children under the age of 18 got engaged in armed groups and even if they did so their roles in armed conflicts were limited and peripheral. The weapons used by the armed groups were heavy and often not easy for a child to operate without rigorous training. Children were in the margins of the conflict and were used mostly as informers, porters and cooks (McKay & Mazurana, 2004).

But this situation has changed. Technological advancements have opened up the prospects of engaging children as front fighters and even those under the age of 18 are being recruited as front fighters, in violation of human rights. In fact, it is not uncommon to find 12 to 14-year-olds in armed groups across the globe. UNICEF (2015) estimates that around 300,000 children under the age of 18 are currently serving as child soldiers, one fourth of whom can be found in the East Asia and Pacific regions (Emmons, 2001).

It is interesting to understand the political economy of involving children in conflicts. Young children are not only more committed and courageous but they eat less and obey more. Children are getting new exposure and are being forced to survive in an environment of insecurity and fear. A teacher in Syria articulated this tragedy as: 'Right now you can ask any child about the different types of weapons and they would be able to name all of them for you; they remember weapons more than lessons' (Save the Children, 2014).

## Conflict and teachers

It is seen that along with students, teachers are often key targets of armed groups. Teachers face threats of kidnapping and ransom and are forced to provide support to armed groups. Teachers are targeted if the warring groups consider teachers as state employees and not their supporters (Save the Children, 2013). For instance, many teachers have been picked from classrooms and school premises and shot dead in Nepal. The number of incidents of kidnapping, torture and 'disappearance' are always more in countries affected with violence. In Rwanda, during the Rwandan genocide, teachers were the primary target when, in 100 days, from 6 April to 16 July 1994, an estimated 800,000 to 1 million Tutsis and some moderate Hutus were slaughtered.

Teachers are responsible for keeping children safe in schools, and they often find it difficult to achieve this in violence-affected pockets. As a result of attacks on school buildings, frequent strikes, destruction of schools and schools closing down, teachers as government employees often face the challenges of being present in schools in these difficult circumstances.

They get into a catch-22 situation. Government officials want teachers to perform their duties to give people a sense of normalcy and also as a sign of state control over the territory. Being in the schools, in the absence of security forces, teachers become more vulnerable. For example, in Cameroon, teachers are reluctant to work in schools in warring zones, especially in schools closer to its border with Nigeria. In the last quarter of November, 2014, Cameroon officials blamed Boko Haram for attacks on schools which resulted in 130 schools near its northern border with Nigeria closing down. Most students have left the area for safer places (Kindzeka, 2014).

Stories from Cambodia to Syria talk of how teachers and children who resisted the armed groups were kidnapped, tortured or killed. Some were murdered by the police force and some by armed groups. In the first six months of 2013 the following instances of attacks on schools were reported from across the world:

- 1 January, five teachers were killed near Swabi in KP province.
- 26 March, school teacher Shahnaz Ali was shot dead near the Afghan border when he was on his way to school.
- 30 March, during shooting and a grenade attack on a school in Karachi, Abdul Rasheed, the school principal was killed. Among the eight injured, four were students. On the same day, in Karachi again, a girls' school was set on fire.
- 5 May, a boys' school was blown up in Baluchistan.
- 9 May, four more schools were set on fire in a spate of attacks in Baluchistan.
- 10 May, a government school was blown up in Swabi in KP province.

- 15 June, a bomb exploded in a bus carrying female students leading to the killing of 11 people while 22 survived with injuries in Quetta in Baluchistan. Gunmen also attacked the hospital where the injured people were taken for treatment.

(Save the Children, 2013)

In Syria, official data from the Ministry of Education reveal that 222 teachers and education personnel have been killed since the beginning of the conflict in 2011. As of September 2015, 4.1 million Syrians had fled the country, and 6.5 million people had been displaced internally. One of every five displaced persons in the world is Syrian (CNN, 2015). A global terrorism database has also been prepared by the University of Maryland which shows the increasing attacks on schools from 2004 onwards.

Pakistan has experienced the highest number of attacks during the four decades. Between 1970 and 2013, more than two-thirds of the terrorist attacks on education institutions in the country were on unoccupied buildings and were aimed at disrupting education processes or as a means of protest against the government by damaging state property.

The increased demands for money, food and shelter by armed groups, perceived threats of abduction and the challenge of being 'neutral' make people migrate to safer places, which adds to the challenges of protection, education and livelihood for the governments. The gravity of the issue of displacement can be understood if one considers the estimates given by UN agencies. Tracking actual numbers of displaced people demands tracking systems across countries but it is believed that more than 43 million people were displaced in recent years because of armed conflict.

Discontinuity and loss of schooling years are also an outcome of forced migration (CWIN, 2007). If the duration of the conflict is short, this loss can be compensated with an accelerated pace of teaching and learning, but in case it is of a longer duration, children rarely return to their native schools.

Migration brings with it its own problems. Maysa, a 14-year-old Syrian girl who now lives in Egypt, confirms the fear that she had of the host community when she says,

> It was very difficult for my father to register us in school. He suffered a lot to get us in. I don't know the details, but he had to go to many government associations for stamps and other things for

registration. They didn't recognise my sixth grade certificate from Syria, so I had to retake my exams using the Egyptian curriculum so that I could register in the seventh grade here.

(Save the Children, 2014)

Another challenge that minority and refugee children face has to do with the new curriculum, as the idea of a national society is reflected in school processes through various components, such as curriculum, textbooks, language and so on.

On the other side, because schools and teachers represent the government at the local level, they come under attack when there is a reaction against the state establishment. In Thailand, for instance, ethnic Malay Muslim insurgent groups have shown anger against the Thai language and curriculum followed in schools in the country. They have attacked schools in far south Thailand to oppose the teaching and practice of Buddhism in schools. According to GCPEA (2014) 59 teachers were assassinated in this region between 2009 and 2012.

## Education, conflict and financial implications

The financial implications of conflict are many, ranging from changing policy priorities in an ad-hoc manner to cutting down budget outlays for social sectors. Schools are a single window of hope for marginalised people, as they perceive education as a tool to move upwards and secure higher levels in society, but conflicts lead to diversion of finances and other resources impacting the curriculum that is taught. The funds that are meant for education and health often are diverted to defence and police services, making children more vulnerable (Roberts, 2005).

Further, donors prefer not to invest in a country which does not have a stable government and a peaceful environment, so funds are transferred to other countries.

In the case of South Sudan, the estimated average cost to repair each of the 21 schools damaged in the 2011 attacks was $67,000. In Syria, the direct cost of replacing damaged, destroyed or occupied schools, replacing lost school equipment and training replacement teachers due to attacks on education has been estimated to be £2.1 billion ($3.2 billion) (Save the Children, 2013).

Ethiopia's education budget is half that of its military budget, and Pakistan spends seven times more on the military than it does on education (UNESCO, 2011, p. 147). One of the reasons for this is a change in government priorities because of reduced economic growth as a result of armed conflicts. This is linked to a reduction in the quality of the services offered by the education and health sectors.

The stability of the government and its mechanisms play a significant role, not only in meeting the genuine demands of people but also in mobilising funds from institutional donors to accelerate developmental work. If the state itself becomes a party to a struggle for its own survival, donors are not attracted to larger commitments towards children and society. The external funding for education gets reduced in cases of conflict. Donor agencies often prefer to fund countries with a stable political situation rather than countries in conflict (Andersen, 2007).

## Classroom implications of conflict

The history of school reveals that the primary reason behind establishing schools was to spread 'cultural homogeneity' among citizens. So, if the public schooling system does not provide space for other identities to be an ingredient of the common identity, the problem will certainly grow. A 11-year-old refugee child, Ahmed, narrated his story, which explains this point: 'The first day at school in Jordan was good. I was excited on the first day. But after one month the teachers started changing. They started hitting us. . . . All the teachers hit us, even the director' (Save the Children International, 2014, p. 27).

In conflicting communities, access to schools may be restricted to particular ethnic groups or communities. A case in point is the education policy in Kosovo during the conflict, where the Serb community tried to remove minority languages from schools in early 1989. All classes where Albanian was the language of instruction were closed down. Serb-orientated curricula was designed and introduced in the schools. The teachers who disagreed were forced to resign (Sommers & Buckland, 2004).

Enmity against an ethnic group has classroom implications as well. The role of the teacher becomes very crucial and could make the situation worse for 'others'. Government officials in Rwanda reported that even a mathematics lesson can be converted to an occasion to create bitterness against some (Bird, 2003). Discriminatory and horrifying classroom practices against a group push children out of school, and children also convert the classroom experience to suit their own meaning of schooling and learning (OECD, 2001).

More often than not, education carries political agendas; therefore, the role of education cannot always be seen as neutral. It could play a positive role in ensuring social harmony among communities, but at the same time, it might also be used to fuel tensions among social groups. For example, classroom practices, the discrimination of one group by the other and the portrayal of one group as 'foreigner' by the other group resulted in genocide in Rwanda. In Rwanda, 70 per cent of the members of the Tutsi minority group were killed during the genocide in the country. Hutu's elite and ruling members perpetrated the killing of almost 20 per cent of Rwanda's total population.

## Gender and conflict

Gender differences are deeply ingrained in social systems and also reflect strongly in schooling processes. Girls are usually assigned less challenging tasks, as they are supposed to be weak and inferior in comparison to boys. This is not only about physical strength; girls are considered as less efficient in their mental abilities as well. They are advised to study subjects that will prepare them for their future roles as homemakers. Parents and the teachers accept a secondary role for girls as 'normal', thus suppressing leadership qualities among them. This gendered identity works to the disadvantage of girls both in school and in the family. Such trends percolate to conflict zones too.

In conflict zones, male members often leave their homes under fear, either to join armed groups or to save their lives. They leave women and children at home, which makes life more challenging for both of these groups. Women and girls left behind often become victims of rape and physical assaults.

While reporting on conflict, journalists hardly notice violations of childen's rights and the engagement of child soldiers, and the term 'child soldiers' is often used for boys. McKay and Mazurana (2004) highlight that in many countries, young girls, too, are forced to join armed groups. In their study, they found confirmed cases of abduction or gang pressing of girls into armed forces or armed opposition groups in 65 per cent of the 39 countries who were under conflict in 2002. Young girls who join armed groups become victims of sexual exploitation and also at times lose their lives. They are exploited not only by people from outside their organisation, but in many cases also by their co-workers, mostly group leaders. Reintegration of these girls into their families and communities is a big challenge. Once peace talks and other related processes start, no one talks about children under 18 years of age, especially about girls who are a part of armed groups.

Conflicts also make girls particularly vulnerable owing to the gendered division of labour; for example, the responsibility for managing household chores rests on their shoulders. Struggle for survival and identity add to their vulnerability.

However, recruiting girls works to the advantage of the armed groups. For example, insurgent groups in Sri Lanka recruited girls because it was economical and strategically important for war lords to have them in their ranks. Girls, too, wanted to join these groups because they were angry with particular ethnic groups or systems, or because they saw this as a means of securing food and shelter for themselves.

It is easy for girls to become a part of armed groups. But their return to normal life is more challenging. Many times girls return with babies, infectious diseases and a sense of guilt for their actions during the armed conflict. The cultural environment also creates hurdles for them when they wish to return to their own communities.

## Quality of education and conflict

The poor quality of learning can also lead to an escalation in conflict, as parents may perceive poor quality education as a discriminatory provision for a particular group (especially the historically excluded). In the case of ongoing conflict, the quality of education is bound to suffer. Many teachers leave their jobs in a conflict situation, resulting in the appointment of untrained teachers, as happened in Bosnia and Herzegovina (Philip, 2004). Untrained teachers are paid less because they have to do additional work other than teaching to meet their financial needs.

# 2 Emergence of Nepal and movements for democracy

Nepal has been a centre of attraction for tourists, historians, political scientists and experts in international affairs for decades. Nepal is now a federal democratic republic with an estimated population of more than 27.8 million (World Bank, 2013) and has a long history, as it emerged from a group of small princely states to a unified nation. The country is located in the Himalayas and is bordered on the north by the People's Republic of China and on the south, east and west by India. Placed at a strategic location between China and India, Nepal is 22 times smaller than India and 75 times smaller than China (Bhattarai, 2003). It covers an area of 147,181 square kilometres and has an average length of 885 kilometres.

## Sociocultural context

Nepal is divided into three economic zones – Mountain, Hills and Terai (plains) – having diverse cultural and linguistic groups. The ecological conditions in the three geographic regions vary from harsh, cold weather in the mountains to humidity in the plains.

A majority of Nepal's citizens are engaged in agricultural activities. The country has an annual population growth rate of 2.24 per cent; 92 languages and dialects has been identified in the country. Nepali is the official language and medium of instruction in government schools. Prior to Nepali, Sanskrit was the medium of instruction in a majority of schools in the 1950s. Maithili, Bhojpuri, Awadhi, Newari, Tharu, Tamang, Magar and Limbu are some of the other linguistic groups of Nepal (Government of Nepal [GoN], 2005).

Nepal has more than 100 ethnic groups, including Chhetris, Hill Brahmins, Magars, Tharus, Tamangs, Newars, Kamis, Yadavs, Rais and Kiratis. Communities in the country have varied educational achievements, and groups like the Hill Brahmins, Newars, Bangalis,

Thakalis, Kyasthas and Maithili Brahmins are considered to be educationally advanced while literacy levels among socially marginalised groups, such as the Doms and Mushahars, are reported to be below 10 per cent. Therefore, a distinct caste divide can be observed in the groups who have had access to education across generations and those who have been barred from it. Often the lower castes have had an opportunity to be 'literate' but not 'educated'.

Nepal had a literacy rate of only 2 per cent in 1951, with 321 primary schools and 11 high schools. The Ministry of Education and Sports reported improved literacy rates of 54 per cent in 2002, with 25,927 primary schools. The number of lower secondary schools reached up to 7,289 while there were 4,350 secondary schools (GoN, 2005).

With more than 25 per cent of the population falling under the poverty line, Nepal belongs to the category of less-developed countries. As reported by UNICEF, gross national income (GNI) per capita in Nepal stands at US $700 (UNICEF, 2014).

The history of Nepal is replete with instances of popular revolts and uprisings against dictatorial rulers and oppressive regimes, especially in the 18th and 19th centuries. The three geographical regions – the Terai, Hills and Mountains – were linked to various dynasties and princely states before unification by King Prithvi Narayan Shah in 1768. National uprisings, however, took place mostly after 1947. Nepal has a long and shared cultural history with India and many Nepali political leaders were part of India's freedom struggle. After India's independence in 1947, Nepali leaders not only formed two major political parties (Nepali Congress and the Communist Party of Nepal) in India but also started their protest against the monarchy. Though political groups experienced a measure of success in the 1950s, significant changes in the political system occurred only as late as the 1990s.

Since 1990, Nepal has appeared more prominently in the news globally and in news in South Asia in particular, as the movement for democracy has gained momentum. The streets of Kathmandu were choked for 18 days in a protest for democracy. People demonstrating on the street returned with an assurance of general elections. The general elections took place after a gap of three decades in 1991. Prior to 1991 all activities by political parties were banned in the country. After the general elections, many coalitions were formed with short-lived governments at the centre, and Nepal had as many as nine prime ministers in one decade! Wobbly governments, fights between mainstream political parties for power and a Kathmandu-centric developmental approach steered the ongoing work of the Communist Party of Nepal (CPN) (the Maoists) on the ground. The long presence of the communists in the historically neglected western regions provided the base for initiating a people's war in 1996. Starting in the Rolpa district in mid-western Nepal, the People's War gradually spread to other regions of the country. Amid this war and the state's fight for survival, media from all over the world gathered in Nepal after the shocking bloodbath at the Palace in 2001, where 16 members of the royal family, including the king, the queen and the crown prince, were murdered.

## Emergence of modern Nepal

It is believed that the Licchivi, Newar, Mall and Khasa dynasties ruled Nepal valley since the 4th century AD. Ari Mall was the first Mall ruler in the 12th century and Yaksh Mall was probably the last ruler of the Mall dynasty, which ruled Kathmandu valley for almost two years. Yaksh Mall had control over Kathmandu, Bhaktpur and Patan in a unified way in 1482.

After Yaksh Mall, Khasas established an empire of 142,000 square kilometres, consisting of a part of the Karnali basin, south-eastern Tibet and parts of Kumaon, but their empire was fragmented at the beginning of the 15th century. The Khasa empire was divided into smaller units of *baisi* (22) in Karnali basin and *chaubisi* (24) in Gandaki region (Whelpton, 2005, pp. 22–23).

Palpa was one of the largest states in the central hills ruled by the Sen dynasty, who in all probability arrived there from north India. After the death of Mukund Sen in 1553, the Kingdom of Palpa was divided, but later a member of the dynasty seized control over Makwanpur and later over Vijaypur states, leading to the expansion of their dominion. Many princely states were in existence during the 17th century and in the first half of the 18th century when their unification was started by Prithvi Narayan Shah, the founder of modern Nepal. Dravya Shah, the ancestor of the erstwhile Shah dynasty, acquired control over Gorkha in 1559. He was the younger brother of the king of the *chaubisi* of Lamjung. The Gorkha kingdom under Dravya Shah's control was a small princely state with 2,000 warriors. Prithvi Narayan Shah ascended the throne in 1743. Being a courageous and visionary personality, Prithvi Narayan Shah mobilised support from Indian Rajputs and took control over Kathmandu, Patan and Bhadgaon kingdoms, which were until then a part of the Mall kingdom. Along with some other small states, he occupied eastern Nepal and some parts of modern Sikkim, and established the Nepal kingdom as a unified state in 1768.

## Emergence of Nepal, movements for democracy

Prithvi Narayan Shah expanded the Nepal kingdom up to the Tibet border before he died in 1775, when the kingdom's expansion was brought to a halt by Qing, a monarch from China in 1792. The Anglo-Nepalese war of 1814–16 resulted in the Sugauli treaty which fixed the boundary of Nepal with India (Whelpton, 2005). In between there were also internal fights for power by family members and courtiers.

> In 1846, Jung Bahadur Rana took over as the Prime Minister after beating his competitors (Pande, Thapa and Basnet) and established the tradition of hereditary Prime Ministership for the Ranas from 1846 to 1953. The hereditary king of the Shah Dynasty became ceremonial as all the powers were exercised by the Ranas (Joshi and Rose 1966). The Ranas held control over the army, administration and external affairs. They isolated Nepal and development work was skewed towards Kathmandu. Several attempts were made to overthrow the Ranas and establish democracy with a constitutional monarchy. One such attempt was led by Jamadar Sripati Gurung of Lamjung in 1875 followed by Lakhan Thapa Magar in 1876. Another group, 'Prachanda Gorkha' had planted a bomb against Rana rulers in Kathmandu but got arrested before the execution of his plan in 1932. Political group Praja Parishad was formed with the aim of getting a constitutional monarchy with democracy in 1935 but four leaders of this group were sentenced to death and others sent to jail on charges of attempting to assassinate the Rana ruler.
>
> (Karki & Seddon, 2003)

The political struggle for development and democracy continued in some form or the other in Nepal but Rana rulers were able to suppress the dissident voices. A small group of allies enjoyed power with the rulers, so formal educational opportunities were also limited to this elite group. Hugh Wood, who was appointed as an educational advisor to the monarch from 1953 to 1959, in fact, remarks that during the Rana regime: 'Schools were forbidden, to seek or offer education was a capital offense' (Sharma, 1990). While the Durbar school educated children of the nobles and the privileged, the common man and his children had no access and opportunity for education. The occasional 'literate youth' that one came across had received some training from a priest or a monk but the institution of schooling was a far cry in the 1960s.

India's independence was a positive reference for political actors as well as Nepali people to put organised pressure on the rulers for a democratic government. Political parties were established and more organised struggle against autocratic Rana rulers of Nepal started after 1947. The CPN was formed in Calcutta in 1947 (Gaige & Scholz, 1991) and Pushpa Lal Shrestha was elected as its leader. An agreement with those engaged in armed struggles as part of the strategy to set up a new democracy and establish a People's Republic were the ideological lines adopted by CPN.

The Nepali Congress Party came into existence in 1948 in Banaras (Upreti, 2008) after the merger of two political groups – the Nepali National Congress (formed in 1947) and the Nepali Democratic Congress (formed in 1948). The Nepali Congress Party agreed to support the armed struggle against the Rana rulers even though leaders of Nepali Congress were followers of the Gandhian principle of non-violence. M.P. Koirala was elected president of the Nepali Congress Party and he planned an armed revolt, and CPN and the Nepali Congress agreed to support an armed struggle against the Rana rulers.

The Ranas were facing challenges created by CPN, Nepali Congress and armed groups, King Tribhuvan was indirectly supporting a constitutional monarch and kept meeting some of the oppositional leaders in Delhi during his stay in India, which he claimed was for medical reasons. In 1950, Nepali Congress launched an armed struggle in the bordering areas of Nepal and attacked the government's garrison at Birganj in which ex-Gurkha servicemen were involved in a majority. Nepali Congress supported rebel group Mukti Sena's initiative resulted in civil unrest in some towns of Terai and Kathmandu valley but their plan of a military takeover reached the Ranas and they arrested a few important military officials. King Tribhuvan was aware of these plans of the Nepali Congress so he was asked by Rana to resign to which he did not agree. The relationship between Rana and the king worsened.

Since the Indian government was also supporting a constitutional monarchy in line with the Nepali Congress and King Tribhuvan, on 6 November 1950, King Tribhuvan left on a hunting trip with his family and took shelter in the Indian embassy at Kathmandu. The Ranas tried to approach King Tribhuvan for a negotiation but he refused to meet the negotiators. Three-year-old Gyanendra (King Tribhuvan's grandson, who had been left behind at the palace) was designated as king by the Ranas and new coins were also issued in his name. The Ranas tried to block the movement of airplanes but on 11 November 1950 the king and his family members arrived in Delhi in an Indian military plane (Cowan, 2015).

The Ranas tried to get international acceptance for their new king but countries like India, the United Kingdom and the United States did not support this arrangement. Over the next two months, pressure on the Ranas was created by political groups Mukti Sena and Nepali Congress, some of the dissenting Ranas and people in general. Protests and agitations started against the Ranas on the streets of Kathmandu and in other cities of Nepal. The Indian government, too, created challenges for the Ranas and finally an agreement was reached between the king, Rana and Nepali Congress for a stable, peaceful and democratic Nepal. With the mediation of the Indian government, consensus was reached for a Rana-Congress coalition government. This conciliation is popularly known as the Delhi Compromise of 1951 (Karki & Seddon, 2003).

King Tribhuvan agreed to act as the constitutional monarch under a new democratic constitution outlined by elected members of the Constituent Assembly. However, once King Tribhuvan got hold of his position, he did not show any willingness to develop a new constitution. Elections were not held for a Constituent Assembly as well. So other than the formation of an interim Rana-Congress coalition government in February 1951, the other points of the Delhi Compromise were not honoured by the rulers (Hutt, 2004).

### First elected democratic government

As a result of the Delhi Compromise, King Tribhuvan was restored to the throne and Padma Shamsher Rana was succeeded by Mohan Shamsher who led the new coalition cabinet for 10 months. Mohan Shamsher was succeeded by Nepali Congress Party leader M.P. Koirala as prime minister in 1951. The differences between King Tribhuvan and Prime Minister M.P. Koirala led to the resignation of M.P. Koirala from his post in 1952. However, he was again invited by the king to be prime minister in 1953. He accepted the offer and continued in office till 1955.

In 1955, King Mahendra succeeded King Tribhuvan, but still no progress was made with respect to the formation of an elected Constituent Assembly. A new constitution was drafted and presented in 1959 by King Mahendra. In this proposed constitution, the king had absolute power to terminate parliament and the cabinet without consulting the Prime Minister. Nepal decided to go for the first parliamentary elections under the new constitution in 1959. Nepali Congress emerged as the single largest party getting 74 out of the 109 seats. The Communist Party of Nepal was divided into two groups on the issue of the perceived role of the monarchy in the country and only won four seats.

Within a year the government run by the Nepali Congress was dissolved by the king who used the new constitutional provisions of 1959 which gave him absolute powers along with military support to dismiss the first elected government of Nepal.

## Ban on political parties

King Mahendra perceived a threat from political parties after dissolving the parliament. Political parties in Nepal approached Indian leaders to garner support in ensuring a constitutional government there. King Mahendra analysed the power dynamics in South Asia and signed a Peace and Friendship treaty with China in 1962. In the same year, the Indo-China war took place in which China emerged as the superior power.

King Mahendra wanted to make use of his association with China and presented a new version of the constitution in 1962. This constitution had a provision for a party-less Panchayat system, which effectively stopped the functioning of political parties in the country. The king held all the powers in the Panchayat system and political parties were banned constitutionally. Freedom of speech and expression was sanctioned by the constitution, but laws did not allow citizens to critique the king publicly. Even local meetings, publications and processions, other than those that were government sponsored, required government approval (Burghart, 1993). The constitution at this time was no more than the will of the ruling elite and served to legitimise a number of autocratic changes in institutions across Nepal.

Nepali Congress and CPN continued their demand for an elected Constituent Assembly and a powerful sovereign parliament (Karki & Seddon, 2003).

King Tribhuvan was succeeded by his son, King Mahendra in 1955. Nepal became a member of the United Nations under his leadership. Considering the new developments and the strategic location of Nepal, the USSR and the United States opened their embassies in Kathmandu in 1958 and 1959, respectively. In 1959, Nepal's first university, Tribhuvan University, was founded in Kathmandu (Khaniya, 2007).

The first constitution of Nepal had been promulgated in 1948 with the Nepal Government Act. The second constitution with modifications was presented in 1951 and a new constitution was introduced in 1959, making provisions for the first general elections under a multi-party system in Nepal (Whelpton, 2005).

Elections were held in Nepal for the first time in 1959. B.P. Koirala of Nepali Congress became the prime minister in 1960 and initiated new developmental policies, which faced huge resistance from the king. King Mahendra unexpectedly dismissed the cabinet and dissolved the parliament (Karki & Seddon, 2003). So the first elected government of Nepal survived only for 18 months (Burghart, 1993). King Mahendra banned all political parties and political activities in 1960.

In 1961, King Mahendra set up a commission to draft a new constitution. The new constitution made provisions for a party-less Panchayat system and made the royal dynasty sovereign. It was promulgated in 1962 by King Mahendra (Hutt, 2004).

Freedom of speech and expression were constitutionally guaranteed during the Panchayat period, but in practical terms these were restricted by laws such as the Treason Act of 1961, which prohibited people critiquing the king publicly. People who dared to criticise the Panchayat system were sent to jail and tortured (Hangen, 2010).

The Panchayat system created a pyramidal structure with villages at its base and the Rastriya Panchayat on the top. Through constitutional amendments, the king appropriated absolute power and became the head of state. All government institutions, cabinet/council of ministers and parliament were made accountable to the king. Several political leaders were sent to jail and many went in exile during the Panchayat period. Prior permission of the government became mandatory for any local meeting, procession or publication other than those sponsored by a state organisation (Burghart, 1993).

The king wanted to project an image of a unified nation state, so in 1962 Nepali was made compulsory as the medium of instruction in all state schools, ignoring other languages. In 1965, Hindi and Newari news broadcasts were terminated on Radio Nepal (Burghart, 1993).

King Birendra ascended the throne after the death of King Mahendra in 1972. Nepal was divided into five developmental regions by the National Development Council. The exiled Nepali Congress leader B.P. Koirala came back to Nepal from India, but the political context was still unfavourable for a multi-party democracy. Koirala was arrested in 1976.

In 1977, at the end of the emergency in India, the Indira Gandhi-led Indian National Congress was defeated. Encouraged by the political developments in India, demonstrations intensified to clear the way for political parties and democracy in Nepal. Facing nationwide demonstrations mainly by students, King Birendra agreed to have a referendum on the Panchayat system.

In 1980, king-supported forces managed to win with a 10 per cent margin in the referendum. Though the Panchayat system continued in Nepal after the referendum, the number of votes cast against the system gave an indication of the eventual emergence of multi-party democracy in the future (Whelpton, 2005). Party-less general elections for the Rastriya Panchayat were held in 1981 and 1986. The Nepali Congress boycotted both elections.

The Nepali Congress staged a civil disobedience (satyagraha) campaign to restore multi-party democracy in 1985 (Whelpton, 2005). In 1986, the second Rashtriya Panchayat elections were held and Marich Man Singh Shrestha became the prime minister and stayed on the post until the mid-1990s. Interestingly, Hoftun (1993) observed that no personal attacks were made on King Birendra by mainstream political parties during the democracy movement as he was regarded as a symbol of national unity.

## Naxal movement in India and influence on Nepal

In India, Charu Mazumdar and Kanu Sanyal tried to follow Mao Tse-Tung's ideology at the ground level in the 1970s. They mobilised youth and labourers against local landlords in the Naxalbari area of West Bengal. The initial success of this movement gained popularity especially among the youth and a group known as Naxalites. The Naxalbari movement became a role model for the communist movement of Nepal and also inspired similar movements in other parts of the world.

Under the influence of the Naxalbari movement, an All Nepal Revolutionary Coordination Committee (ML) was established in eastern Terai. The organisation initiated underground guerrilla war in Jhapa in May 1971.

The Jhapa guerrilla movement (People's War) was the first organised attempt by Nepali revolutionary communists to implement Mao's ideology and his revolutionary strategy on the ground.

The Jhapa movement became popular in India and got extended support from youth activists in other parts of the country as well. However, this tide of insurgency was stemmed by the police, leading to the death of many activists. After being encountered by the police force in 1971, the All Nepal Revolutionary Coordination Committee (ML) regrouped in 1978 with a new name – the Nepal Communist Party (Marxist-Leninist) – and modified its political strategy with an emphasis on analysing economic and social conditions in Nepal and charting their own path to socialism.

NCP (Marxist-Leninist) leaders Pushpa Lal Shrestha, Mohan Bikram Singh and Nirmal Lama were in agreement that a protracted war was the only path to a democratic system in the country. However, on the issue of an alliance with Nepali Congress and other political forces to put down the monarch, radical leaders had differences of opinion.

Differences emerged on the ideological lines of Marxism and Maoism along with pro-Soviet and pro-China stands by the leaders.

Mohan Bikram Singh and Nirmal Lama of CPN (4th Congress in September 1974) adopted a strategy to initiate a people's movement which could be converted into an armed revolt at an appropriate time. The group's ideological line and strategy became the foundation for the current leaders of CPN (Maoist) in Nepal.

The death of Mao in China (1976) led to intense political discussions within the communist block of Nepal and by 1983–84, CPN (4th Congress) was divided into two groups – CPN (Masal) led by Mohan Bikram Singh and CPN (4th Congress) led by Nirmal Lama. CPN (Masal) again fragmented into two groups with almost similar names – CPN (Masal) which was led by Mohan Bikram Singh and Baburam Bhattarai. Another fraction CPN (Mashal) was represented by Mohan Baidya along with Pushpa Kamal Dahal 'Prachanda' who became general secretary of the party in 1989 (Muni, 2004).

In 1990, Prachanda managed to bring together all the CPN factions (4th Congress) (except Mohan Bikram's CPN-Masal) and formed CPN (Unity Centre).

On the other side, some sections of the Nepali Congress continued their activities against the king and the Panchayat system. During this period (1972–74), several violent incidents took place, including an attempt to assassinate King Birendra, a passenger plane being hijacked, bombings in some places and armed insurgency in Timburbote. Some frequent protests and mobilisation of people on the ground were continued by Nepali Congress leaders in these years as well. As the satyagraha (civil disobedience) campaign and general strikes were started by Nepali Congress in 1985, communist groups began a *jail bharo* (fill the jails) movement demanding elections of a Constituent Assembly and of making Nepal a republic.

When these movements started gaining ground, there were a series of bomb blasts in Kathmandu and Pokhara in 1986. An India-based Nepal Janbadi Morcha (People's Front) led by Ram Raja Prasad Singh (he became the presidential candidate from CPN [Maoists] in 1998) took responsibility for the bombings saying that they wanted to bring down the monarchy and abolish private property in Nepal.

Some people were of the opinion that the bombs were planted by the palace to disrupt the political movement initiated by Nepali Congress and communist groups. Taking advantage of the bomb blasts, mass arrests took place and Nepali Congress called off the satyagraha campaign.

## Democracy movement of 1990: an initiative of the United Front

Prime Minister Marich Man Singh Shrestha was unable to renegotiate the Trade and Transit treaty with India in March 1989. In May 1989, India banned free trade borders with Nepal. This blockade (March 1989 to July 1990) resulted in an economic crisis and price hikes in consumable goods in Nepal (Karki & Seddon, 2003). There was a crisis of essential services, which led to resentment. This prepared a base for political movements against the Panchayat system in Nepal.

In 1989, a unification process started to bring all of the eleven communist factions of Nepal under one umbrella, and by 1990, seven factions had come together as the United Left Front, which came together with Nepali Congress to form a United Front in 1990. Mainstream political parties agreed to initiate a joint movement to make the struggle decisive despite their ideological differences. United Front of Nepali Congress and seven left parties launched nationwide protests for 18 days in April 1990 demanding restoration of multi-party democracy and the abolition of the Panchayat system (Hoftun, 1993). There were demonstrations, protests, marches on the streets and public confrontations with the police. *Jail bharo* became a successful formula as prisons in the country overflowed with political activists (Burghart, 1993).

The police tried to control the protesters by force. Many people were killed by police fire; many more were injured and jails were packed during the movement. All primary and secondary schools and Tribhuvan University were shut down. A larger number of teachers played a significant role in mobilising the public on the streets. People facing economic challenges, and harbouring a reactionary attitude towards the administration because of the way in which it was dealing with the protestors, resulted in more public support for political parties. A well-coordinated team of the Nepali Congress and UML leaders channelised the public anger efficiently. Protests intensified into a mass movement, which became a turning point in the contemporary history of Nepal.

Protests on the streets of Kathmandu became intensified and were noticed by the world media. On 16 April 1990, King Birendra announced that he had agreed to participation of political parties, making changes to the constitution of 1962 and ending the 29-year-old Panchayat system (Upreti, 2008). This movement of 1990 is popularly known as the Democracy Movement in Nepal (Raeper & Hoftun, 1992), and it became the foundation for the republic of Nepal. This new development provided space for political groups to work freely with communities and to organise political activities. People also found a platform to raise their voices and grievances through political parties.

As the king agreed to replace the Panchayat system with multi-party political democracy, political parties succeeded in forming an interim government on 7 May 1990. After six months, an improved version of the constitution became effective on 9 November 1990 with provisions for multi-party legislative elections in 1991.

In May 1990 an interim government was formed, consisting of representatives of Nepali Congress, the Left Front and representatives of the king. K.P. Bhattarai of Nepali Congress became the prime minister of the interim government.

Nepali Congress and Left Front became part of the interim government in May 1990 but revolutionary groups (Masal, Mashal and Revolutionary Workers Party) were in favour of continuing the movement so that the monarchy could be eliminated and elections could be held for the Constituent Assembly. So they continued street protests under Samyukta Rastriya Janaandolan (United National People's Movement) in favour of a Constituent Assembly even after the interim government had been formed.

## Multi-party legislative elections, 1991

Multi-party legislative elections were held in Nepal for the second time after a gap of three decades in May 1991 (Whelpton, 1993) and both the leading political parties, Nepali Congress and the Communist Party of Nepal (UML), of the 1990 movement performed well in the general elections of 1991. The Nepali Congress emerged as the single largest party with 110 seats, the CPN-UML (United Marxist Leninist) got 69 seats and the CPN (Unity Centre)-supported United People's Front of Nepal (UPFN) won 9 seats (Whelpton, 1993).

Baburam Bhattarai was the coordinator of UPFN, and Prachanda was the leader of CPN (Unity Centre). In this election, the Nepali Congress President and interim Prime Minister K.P. Bhattarai was defeated by CPN-UML leader Madan Bhandari. Girija Prasad Koirala of the Nepali Congress became the prime minister after the 1991 general elections.

The revolutionary group CPN (Unity Centre) under the leadership of Prachanda went underground and supported its front organisation – the United People's Front of Nepal (UPFN) in the 1991 elections. Baburam Bhattarai led the UPFN in the elections and managed to win just nine seats.

In 1993, CPN-UML leader Madan Bhandari was found dead in a mysterious car accident and CPN-UML staged countrywide demonstrations to bring down the G.P. Koirala's government. Differences emerged among the leaders of the Nepali Congress and the party was divided. During a vote on the no-confidence motion, 36 members of the Nepali Congress were absent from Parliament. G.P. Koirala could not gather support from enough members and resigned. Nepal went for mid-term elections in November 1994.

## Mid-term elections in 1994: formation of the first communist government

In the 1994 elections, Nepali Congress stood second and CPN-UML emerged as the single largest party in a hung parliament. The first communist government was formed in Nepal, but it faced a crisis in 1995 and was dissolved.

## Making of CPN (Maoist)

In contrast to mainstream political parties, United National Peoples' Movement (UNPM) rejected the new constitution promulgated in November 1990 and decided to continue its work on the revolutionary front. Pushpa Kamal Dahal, aka Prachanda, was leading the Communist Party of Nepal (Unity Centre-Ekta Kendra) and supported the frontal organisation the United People's Front of Nepal (UPFN) on political and electoral fronts. It was agreed within the party that CPN (Unity Centre) would go underground to work on the revolutionary front and UPFN would be visibly active. It seems that the party wanted to try both the options so that it could switch fronts depending on the situation at hand.

In 1992, local elections were held in which Nepali Congress performed well followed by UML and others. UPFN performed poorly in the elections and started a nationwide strike and violence. Prior to the mid-term elections in 1994, CPN (Unity Centre) was divided into two groups – CPN (Unity Centre) led by Mohan Bikram Singh and Nirmal Lama and CPN (Maoist) led by Prachanda. UPFN also got divided on similar lines – the Baburam Bhattarai faction supported Prachanda and the group led by Niranjan Govind Vaidya supported CPN (Unity Centre) of Mohan Bikram Singh and Nirmal Lama.

The UPFN faction led by Baburam Bhattarai was not recognised by the election commission (the Vaidya group was) so it decided to boycott the 1994 elections. Baburam Bhattarai's UPFN group started the groundwork to ensure revolutionary changes through armed struggles rather than through the parliamentary democratic system along with CPN (Maoist).

The formal announcement of the Nepal Communist Party (Maoist) was made in March 2005 and the party adopted a strategy of protracted war to establish a new democracy in the country (Upreti, 2008). The Nepal Communist Party (Maoist) started opposing mainstream political parties, advocating the exit of the monarchy and working towards establishing a People's Republic in Nepal.

## Preparing the ground for the People's War

CPN (Maoist) was already working to strengthen its support base and developing cadres in some pockets of the western region. In Rolpa and Rukum districts of the western hills they enjoyed a lot of support from the people. These places were suitable for guerrilla war and were not well connected by communication channels. Because they were remote, these districts were underdeveloped and hard to reach by the administration. On the international front, CPN (Maoist) became a member of the Revolutionary Internationalist Movement (RIM) and gained encouragement and support from outside Nepal also.

A majority of the people in the mid-western region were extremely poor and socially marginalised, so Maoists got extended support from them. This, along with conducive surroundings, helped them launch an armed struggle from Rolpa and Rukum districts. The districts were considerably isolated from Kathmandu and geographical conditions were suitable for guerrilla war as the region had preferred communists over other political players, including the king since the 1950s.

Violent activities started with the looting of banks, attacks on government offices and kidnapping of people in the area. Cases with criminal charges were filed against UPFN activists and a counter operation, 'Operation Romeo', was launched by the government to crackdown on the Maoist hold in the region. UPFN demanded suspension of the government officials from Rolpa and Rukum because of the police atrocities. CPN (Maoist), with an increased support base in the far western region, planned to set up a 'People's Government' in some districts in 1995 (Manchanda, 2006).

The wide economic gap between the ruling class and others, extreme poverty, poor quality of education and unemployment contributed to fuelling the conflict. Exclusion of the socially marginalised groups was visible to a great extent in all aspects of life, government, politics, etc. Their grievances, long-pending demands and the feeling of relative deprivation among the common people were used by the Maoists very strategically. Ethnic groups, which had a desire for equal opportunities and quality services in education and health, were channelised by political actors in order to dethrone the monarchy.

## Beginning of the People's War

A 40-point charter of demands was presented before the Sher Bahadur Deuba-led government by UPFN/CPN (Maoist) in January 1996. They gave one month's time to the government to respond to the demands (by 17 February 1996). The Maoist leaders communicated that if the government did not respond to their demands positively, UPFN/CPN (Maoist) would initiate an armed struggle against the state. In fact, they had been working on this idea for a long time and had prepared the ground by 1994–95 but had wanted a 'justifiable' reason to opt for a path of armed struggle. Many of their demands were basically copied from the 1991 UPFN election. Some demands were vaguely related to socioeconomic disparities in Nepali society and some others were linked to the Indo-Nepal relationship.

Before the end of the one-month's notice, leaders of CPN (Maoist) announced the People's War against the state on 13 February 1996. They had prepared the cadres and strategy for the war so they could not wait until the end of their notice period for the government's response. The People's War was initiated with the objective of establishing a People's Republic in Nepal and the abolition of the monarchy (Muni, 2004; Karki & Seddon, 2003).

The People's Liberation Army was formed and the Maoists established a parallel government in some districts. Schools, banks and government offices were attacked and looted (Varma, 2005). Joshi and Mason (2011) have raised a thought-provoking question on Maoists getting support from farmers: 'How a party can succeed in mobilizing peasants for the dangerous enterprise of armed insurgency when it could not persuade them to commit to the far less risky political act of voting for its candidates in democratic elections?' Perhaps the peasants realised the importance of revolutionary politics over multi-party democracy as they had observed short-lived unstable governments after the end of the Panchayat system in 1990.

Increased unemployment, economic disparities and the rural-urban divide further added to people's resentment. Rich people had become richer and the poor had become poorer in the last two decades of the 20th century. Like education, poverty reduction was also closely linked with the social structure, as the poverty reduction rate was much better among Bahun and Chetri groups (46 per cent) than it was in the Dalit groups (21 per cent) during the 10 years of the People's War (Tiwari cited in Lawoti, 2010).

Poor education, health services and reduced agriculture production forced communities into poverty. The prices of commodities kept increasing, but wages for landless labourers did not improve proportionately during the Panchayat period (Macfarlane, cited in Lawoti, 2010) so people who were facing harsh poverty were promised better services and equal opportunities by Maoists. This helped the Maoists to get the support of the socially and economically deprived groups.

## Expansion of the media and awareness of common issues

The expansion of media and communication technology after the end of the Panchayat period played a significant role in generating awareness around political rights (Gaige & Scholz, 1991). A Buddhist Monk in Lumbini, and others in Delhi, explained that during the Panchayat system, the private media was banned and the government had its own radio and publications. After the restoration of multi-party democracy in the 1990s, private media houses got opportunities to start FM radios, TV channels and newspapers. These new avenues provided space to articulate multiple political perspectives and demands. Awareness levels increased, as people started seeing developments in other countries and started comparing these with their own context. The phenomenal growth of the media generated debates on ideological lines and helped citizens come closer to each other.

## Wider world view and enhanced aspirations

The contribution of youth and adolescent groups was crucial in the transition of the country from the Panchayat system to a democratic republic. A majority of the youngsters contributed not only through rallies, protests and street demonstrations but they also joined armed groups and awareness generation campaigns. In contrast to earlier generations, boys and girls born after the 1970s had more exposure to the outside world and to new technologies. A sizeable number of them went to study and work in other countries and came back with a desire to see a modern Nepal and so joined the anti-king forces.

Educated family members of elites in villages and towns returned from universities with strong sympathies for either the Nepali Congress or the communists and used their prestige to influence village politics.

Even non-sympathisers living in remote government posts cooperated with the Communists for pragmatic reasons and provided indirect support through prestige, bureaucratic favours, information and monetary contributions during the elections (Gaige & Scholz, 1991). Youth associated with development agencies/NGOs also got oriented to a rights' based perspective while working with local and international organisations. Students revealed that through cultural events organised by political parties, people realised the importance of democracy and development in the country and came forward to support the change of guard.

## Sociopolitical exclusion and injustice

Exclusion and injustice are very deep-rooted issues in Nepal. The nature of exclusion is complex and in many cases goes beyond gender and caste and opens many dimensions for debate. Regional disparities also exist, but Kathmandu valley enjoyed preferences at the expense of other regions. Most of the investment activities (in the hotel industry, vehicles, power, etc.) before the 1990s, were concentrated around Kathmandu, where only 5 per cent of the population resided (Whelpton, 2005).

The people of Nepal continued to experience challenges on social and economic fronts. Leaving aside the issue of quality in basic services in social sectors like health and education, the mere availing of these services was not easy for ordinary people before the larger political change. As many as 11 of the 75 districts did not have a single public hospital and on an average one doctor was appointed to serve a population of 14,000 people until 1993–1994 (NESAC cited in Lawoti, 2010, p. 21).

Gender, social category and regional identity were also considerable factors in social and political life. Discrimination occurred in public institutions. One of the leaders of the Sadbhavana Party (Anandi Group) raised the issue of Madhesi representation in the Nepal Army. The Terai accounted for almost one-third of the population with relatively greater educational background, but had meagre representation in the bureaucracy and the army (Burghart, 1993). The people of the regions sharing borders with India were perceived to be more faithful to India by a section of the elites. This was largely because the people in these regions shared the same physical features and language with the people in Uttar Pradesh and Bihar in India. Availing of health and education services in India was easier for the people of the Terai. However, they were treated as 'Nepali' in India and as 'Madhesi' in Nepal.

They were also discriminated against in recruitments both in the Nepalese as well as the Indian army. Long pending grievances of regional disparities and discrimination on social and ethnic backgrounds helped political groups to gather people.

Discrimination against women was also widespread and life was difficult for both widows and single women. Citizenship was given naturally to male members of a family but for a girl, commendation was necessary from her father or husband.

In education and other sectors, such as media, politics, bureaucracy and development, upper caste representation was almost 75 per cent, which confirms that social origin-based differences failed to converge over time despite the expansion of educational services. Caste stratification was also reflected in the literacy levels of social groups (Haq, 1992; Sharda, 1977; Smith & Cheung, 1986). Social inequality was very strongly reflected in economic and job opportunities and levels of education attainment.

The political scenario was also a mirror of the stratified society in Nepal, and the leadership of all political parties was in the hands of upper caste groups. Even after the end of the Panchayat system and restoration of multi-party democracy, creating space for excluded groups was a challenge. Only one Dalit was elected to the House of Representatives in a 13-year span (1990–2002) under multi-party democracy (Lawoti, 2010).

## Bureaucracy and slow decision-making processes

The lethargic bureaucracy of the king was known for delaying work, rather than for working for the people. *Bholi Aunuhosa* (Come tomorrow) and *Mathi Sodhanu Parchha* (Needs to be referred to the supervisors) were frequent responses by the officials to the general public (Rana, 1998). Only the kith and kin of the privileged were favoured by the bureaucracy. Officials were involved in corruption and could not improve essential services.

The effects of slow decision making were visible in the distribution of textbooks, recruitment and training of teachers as well as in delayed allocation of funds to schools. The education system faced issues of slow and corrupt processes like most other government agencies. The absence of an effective judicial system, lack of transparency and long-pending grievances were some of the reasons that people started losing faith in government systems.

The Maoists initiated the People's Court as a governance tool that affected a large number of people. Through the People's Court (Jan

Adalat), the Maoists resolved long-pending property disputes in villages (Kattel, 2003). Quick decisions and punishment for 'culprits' (and most of such decisions were pro-poor) sent a message to the masses, who were distressed with oppressive institutions and individuals. These factors generated support for the movement aimed at changing the political and bureaucratic culture in the country.

## Teachers: the backbone of the Maoist movement

Even the spread of education after 1950 and after the 1990s did not help in social convergence and reducing economic gaps between social groups, but professional groups of teachers and students stood as the backbone of the People's War (Muni, 2004). The socially excluded groups were lagging behind on every front so teachers and students helped CPN (Maoists) to disseminate their ideology and programmes in rural and urban areas.

Teachers and students not only added an intellectual flavour to the movement but also generated debates on existing hierarchies, values, economic inequalities and widespread sociocultural disparities. They worked as a bridge between the leaders and the community. In search of a suitable platform, many ethnic groups aligned with the People's War. Teachers played a catalytic role, and students, jobless youth and landless labourers contributed to the revolution with a dream of breaking the historical cycle of exclusion and of transforming the country.

Grievances were articulated well by the Maoists after 1990 at the national, regional and village levels and they also got political space with the Nepali Congress, CPN (UML) and others. Many larger demands (education in the mother tongue; equal opportunities without discrimination on the basis of gender, caste, religion; free education up to the secondary level) of the communities were part of the 40-point charter submitted by the Maoists to the prime minister in 1996, just before the launch of the People's War (Muni, 2004). Teachers and students helped in spreading the organisational base of the party, as the All Nepal National Independent Student's Union (ANNISU) claimed that it had 600,000 members including children in primary schools during the movement (Harris quoted in Muni, 2004).

In a country where the king, who was the authority of the state, was in confrontation with political and armed groups and was fighting for his own survival till the end of 2006, children and teachers could not remain unaffected. Children and teachers were active actors in the transition process and were also victims of circumstances.

The Maoists propagated the uselessness of parliamentary politics and suggested a revolutionary path to make Nepal a democratic and developed nation. The People's War spread to six districts – Rukum, Rolpa, Jajarkot, Salyan, Gorkha and Sindhuli.

CPN (Maoist) commandos captured some police stations and government offices and looted money from a bank in February 1996. They destroyed the loan documents that farmers kept in the bank (Varma, 2005).

The support base of CPN (Maoist) extended further into other areas, and parallel local governments were established in nine autonomous areas (Manchanda, 2006). The police tried to confront the Maoists by randomly picking up people in these areas. Random arrests and torture by the police lead to enhanced support for the Maoists. Police moved to the cities leaving neutral people and employees at the mercy of the Maoists.

When Nepal was going through a transition from one political system to another, it was not possible for various institutions to remain unaffected. Schools and the school system were no exception in the decade of the People's War. The political journey from the Panchayat system to multi-party democracy and the departure of monarchy has had a great impact on Nepal. Teachers and students have emerged as lead contributors in the transition, with a long and eventful political drive.

## Third general elections in 1999

With the rise and fall of many coalitions between 1995 and 1997, the Nepali Congress and RPP coalition managed the government till 1999. The third general election (after the abolition of the Panchayat system) was held in 1999 and Nepali Congress became the single largest party with absolute majority in parliament. Once again, K.P. Bhattarai became the prime minister of Nepal; he was replaced by Girija Prasad Koirala in 2000 to lead the 9th government in the 10-year span of multi-party democracy.

Unfortunately, the governments that were formed post the 1990s could not become stable and failed to implement radical socioeconomic programmes. People who supported political parties during the democracy movement started losing hope and trust. With frequent changes in leadership and short-lived governments, the mainstream political parties lost credibility, which resulted in resentment against the political parties and the elected government (Karki, 2003).

CPN (Maoists) tried to channelise this aggravation against political parties and the monarchy and entered the People's War in 1996. In

2001, the murder of King Birendra, his queen, crown prince Deependra and some other members of the royal family in a mysterious situation contributed to making Nepal a chaotic state. The People's War continued and Gyanendra became the new king. He tried to hold absolute power in 2005, thus angering all the major political parties. Seven political parties got together to form an alliance to bring the king down. A peace agreement was signed with CPN (Maoists) in 2006 and finally monarchy ended in the country in 2007, after a period of 234 years.

# 3 State and education provisions in the backdrop of the People's War

The history of education in Nepal starts with religious education, which was linked to social hierarchy, the beneficiaries of which were children of upper caste families. The intention behind this religious education was to make pupils become priests and perform *karmkand*. This religious education had two powerful streams, which were led by the Hindu priests and Buddhist monks (UNESCO, 1984). A gender divide was implicit in this form of education, as girls could not perform these ceremonies and their participation was therefore limited.

Religious headships and institutions were supported by the rulers and they exercised authority over the common people. Being an underdeveloped country ruled by monarchy for almost 234 years, followed by unstable governments, the even otherwise limited educational opportunities were confined to a limited group of people and were not widely spread and universal. Young scholars were educated in temples and gombas for religious roles according to Hindu and Buddhist practices, respectively. The Sanskrit education system minimised the Buddhist influence on the education system. Later, the modern education system initiated in India had a huge influence on Nepal (Nepal National Education Planning Commission, 1956).

The government appointed the Education Commission of 1954 to review the school system and make suggestions for educational reforms (Nepal National Education Planning Commission, 1956). This commission was the first organised attempt to prioritise education in the country. The commission recognised the issues of limited access to schools and the challenges of getting teachers, as they are essential for developing new schools. Dr Hugh Wood, an educational advisor appointed by the monarch, speaks at length of the myriad issues involved in establishing a formal educational structure from scratch in Nepal in the early 1950s. Apart from the scarcity of educated people who could serve as teachers, Wood also speaks of 'mobility inertia' as a result of which educated youth from Kathmandu were disinterested in settling in the peripheries of the empire to teach there. The local people were equally unwelcoming of these urban strangers. Infrastructural deficiencies like lack of classrooms, books and teaching aids were other problems, and the entire responsibility fell on teachers to ensure that despite the circumstances students were educated.

In the decades since then the number of schools has gone up and the basic character of school education, too, has changed slowly with political will and people's demand. The revised Constitution of Nepal (1990) gave the right to education to all children. Some major changes have been observed in all areas of school education as Nepal has become a democratic republic with the end of the People's War in 2006.

## Education system in Nepal in the modern times

Although Nepal was relatively isolated from the world during the Rana period (1846–1951), with insignificant economic developments, the first formal school was established during this period. Ranas, being representatives of the ruling class, wanted to educate their children so that they could interact with people from outside, but they were suspicious and hesitant to expand education for common citizens (Shakya, 2003, p. 19). Jung Bahadur Rana made the provision of a home tutor for the royal children in 1854. Gradually this tutorial system got converted into a palace school, accommodating children of other elites. In 1883, this school became the first formal school of modern education in Nepal and was known as the Darbar High School. However, this school was not open to ordinary children and exclusively served the members of ruling families and their courtiers. This was the beginning of the English medium education system in Nepal (UNESCO, 1984).

Access to an English medium school and western curriculum with Nepali and Sanskrit languages in the Darbar High School kept the children of ruling classes ahead of the others, further strengthening the gap between the ruling classes and the common people (Bista, 1991, p. 119).

Ruling elites of Nepal were willing to protect and project 'Nepali' identity, especially to differentiate themselves from India and to promote unity among the citizens. So along with English medium education for their own children, Nepali and Newari languages were promoted; these also had cultural traits. This aspiration became more obvious later when Nepali was made the medium of instruction in all schools in Nepal.

When Dev Shumsher Rana took charge in 1901, he started 200 Nepali medium primary schools in the country. This was a very progressive step, but he faced criticism and was overthrown. Many schools could not survive after four months. The proposal to making Nepali an official language came into being in 1934 when it was declared the official language for all (Nussbaum, 2007). Gradually, education became a necessity for jobs and it also became an indicator of social status.

Religion and education have always been linked in Nepal. Nepali rulers preferred not to send their educated children to the United Kingdom or the United States for higher education in the early 20th century because of religious fears. It was believed that the children would come in contact with impure non-Hindu people and would face challenges in finding local food there. This was an indication that education in Nepal would continue with a special political, social and religious identity.

The first school showed the way for the structure of school education in the country, with classes classified as lower primary (1st and 2nd standard), upper primary (3rd to 5th standard), middle school (6th to 8th standard) and high school (9th and 10th standard). Some 'language' schools were also started, which later became Sanskrit schools. In the 1940s, Gandhi's Basic Education (*Buniyadi Siksha*) system was proposed in India. This had an influence on Nepal and 21 schools had been established on the lines of *Buniyadi Siksha* by 1954, but by 1961 these schools had been converted to regular primary schools (UNESCO, 1984).

Recognising teachers as the cornerstone for education, the first teacher training institute for basic education was started in 1949 in Kathmandu. In four years, the institute provided training to teachers in 55 schools (Nepal National Education Planning Commission, 1956). However, the institute could not be sustained after 1953, and teachers were not given the option of being trained.

During the 1950s and 1960s, most of the schools were a result of community initiatives and were considered 'village schools' (usually up to class 2). Schools with classes higher than the 2nd standard were usually located in larger towns and were attached to high schools. Most of the village schools were 'one-room-one-teacher schools' (Nepal National Education Planning Commission, 1956). In 1950, only 330 primary schools were functional in Nepal and the total literacy rate was only 5 per cent (Whelpton, 2005).

In the absence of government support, tuition fees were the major source of income for running the schools. School fees ranged from 50 paisa to Rs 6 per child per month. Unaided schools were neither free, nor open to everyone. They were highly selective and removed from the normal life of Nepali communities (Nepal National Education Planning Commission, 1956).

## Nepal's education system, 1951–1960

Schooling for the general people expanded only after 1951, when a popular movement ended the autocratic Rana family regime and initiated a democratic system (Whelpton, 2005). Immediately afterwards, the thirst for education could be seen even in remote areas, bringing with it a commitment towards education on the part of the communities.

The first elected government of Nepal established 1,600 primary schools in a single year, followed by 600 more primary schools in the next year. The schools were also opened keeping in mind the need for establishing polling booths for the state elections in addition to recognising the importance of education for the people (Acharya, 2002).

Many communities started schools for educating their children. Most schools were managed jointly by the teachers and the community. The role of the government in these schools was limited to providing nominal financial support. This support was dependent on the availability of funds. According to both officials and teachers, educated youth offered to teach voluntarily or with a nominal remuneration in the hope that they would be accommodated in the system later. Consequently, while the network of schools grew, it did not receive the necessary support from the state, resulting in less than optimum progress.

Ironically, in 1955 when King Mahendra sacked the democratically elected government of Nepal and introduced the party-less Panchayat system, he argued that Nepali people were not literate enough to participate in direct parliamentary elections. He put a ban on all political activities and started consolidating his position so as to be able to deal with political pressure. Subsequent rulers also considered education and awareness among people as more of a threat than a contribution to the development of the country. No systematic attempts were made by the monarchs to expand education for rural children beyond primary and lower secondary levels. It is not surprising that many Nepali leaders and a substantial number of officials and teachers had studied in India and were influenced by the democratic processes that came into practice after 1947.

The education system was used as a way of consolidating the rule and ideology of the new regime. Followed by a change in the political system in Nepal, the Nepal National Education Planning Commission initiated the development of a National Education System in 1954–1955 with a focus on developing a unified Nepal.

The commission focused on achieving the target of ensuring free primary education (up to 5th standard) by 1985 (UNESCO, 1984). It also highlighted the issue of limited expansion of education and concentration of schools mainly in the towns (Nepal National Education Planning Commission, 1956).

The commission suggested initiating 'National Primary Schools' as a uniform public-supported education system. It recommended a revised curriculum and suggested that the following subjects should be included in it for 3rd to 5th standard: Nepali, social science, arithmetic, art education, health and physical education, science, vocational Education and English (UNESCO, 1984). The government accepted the suggestions of establishing national schools. However, privately owned English medium schools grew faster in number than government primary schools.

Caddell (2007) quotes from an official document of the Ministry of Education Nepal (MoE, 1956) which shows that the ruler realised that he could not deny education any more, especially after getting rid of an elected government and controlling absolute power. The document says:

> We have become part of the world, whether we like it or not. We can no longer remain isolated; the world has come to us. How can we meet this world without education? Must we – who once were the crossroads of civilisation – bow our heads in shame to our worldly visitors? How can we evaluate the 'gifts' that are offered us – ideologies, new customs, inventions and the ways of a new strange world? How can we protect ourselves against slogans and ideologies detrimental to the interests of our country? We can do none of these without education to give us understanding and strength to lead us.

## Nepal's education system, 1960–1970

In 1961, another commission – the All-round National Education Commission – was set up to study the education system and suggest reform measures (UNESCO, 1984).

Through this commission, in 1962 the king introduced Nepali as a medium of instruction in all government-supported schools, without giving flexibility to regional languages (Burghart, 1993). The commission suggested dropping English from primary schools and the government accepted this recommendation as well. These changes were done with a vision of making Nepal a unified state and establishing supremacy of the Hill-dominated Nepali identity in a multilingual and multicultural country. The slogan *Ek bhasa, ek besh, ek desh* (one language, one attire, one country) was propagated to reiterate patriotism and honesty towards the monarchy (Nussbaum, 2007). With emphasis on Nepali and Nepali identity, Newari and Hindi news broadcasts on Radio Nepal were stopped in 1965 (Burghart, 1993).

In 1970, vocational education was introduced in 29 high schools and after a year vocational education became a compulsory subject in all high schools in the country (MoE, 1956).

Efforts were made to implement a free and compulsory education model in Jhapa and Chitwan districts and in some town Panchayats with 25 per cent contribution from the government. However, this model got into a financial crisis and could not be sustained (UNESCO, 1984).

The Curriculum, Textbooks and Supervision Development Centre (CTSDC) was set up as a unit under the Ministry of Education and Culture to prepare the curriculum and design textbooks for all grades during the Panchayat period. Textbooks were selected by a committee and the writer received a monetary reward if his or her book was selected.

## State of education, 1970–1980

The introduction of the New Education System Plan (NESP) in 1971 ensured increased government financing of education. Under the system, all schools running in partnership with the community were taken over by the government (Acharya, 2002). Consequently, the department of education became the controlling authority (Whelpton, 2005). Teachers became government employees, and the role of the community was reduced. Universalisation of primary education then became the government's stated policy.

NESP was aligned with the ideologies and values of the Panchayat system. The focus was to develop a skilled workforce for the economic development of the country. Theoretically, NESP aimed at improving the quality of education and promoting vocational education at the school level. NESP could not be fully implemented on the ground because of a resource crunch (Acharya, 2002).

NESP could not deliver quality education nor provide access to education to poorer families. As NESP was not a success, privatisation continued to increase. The literacy rate increased gradually, but the quality of learning in government schools was under question.

However, Sanskrit continued as a school subject and as a medium of instruction in the Sanskrit *pathsaalas* (schools). Private schools had English as a medium of instruction until 1974. With the Education System Plan of 1974, Nepali language was made a compulsory medium of instruction in government primary schools as well. The reason provided was to avoid growing social tensions between Nepali medium students and English medium students and to promote unity among the citizens. Nussbaum (2007) highlights the fact that 'the emphasis on Nepali both differentiated the country from India and became a marker of internal unity and sameness' (2007, p. 268).

On 24 February 1975, on the occasion of his coronation, King Birendra declared primary education to be free. Later, textbooks up to 3rd standard were also made available for free. Later, with the inclusion of the 4th and 5th standards in primary schooling, the provision of providing free textbooks was extended up to 5th standard (UNESCO, 1984). A nationalised system of textbook production was put in place, but expansion of schools without infrastructure and trained teachers led to poor quality of teaching and learning. This led to high dropout rates and stagnation.

The structure of schooling before 1981 was:

> Primary (1st–3rd standard), lower secondary (4th–7th standard), secondary (8th–10th standard).

The structure adopted after 1981 was:

> Primary (1st–5th standard), lower secondary (6th–7th standard), secondary (8th–10th standard).

In 1975, there were 18,874 teachers working in primary schools; their number had increased to 27,805 by 1980 (UNESCO, 1984). Two-thirds of them were untrained teachers.

For a primary school teacher, a school leaving certificate (SLC), qualification equivalent to 10th standard and one year of training at the Institute of Education was required. For lower secondary school, the eligibility was an SLC and a two-year teacher's training course. There was another teacher's training course (B Level) for those who had not completed SLC and were willing to teach in primary schools. Some courses in teacher's training were facilitated through radio and distance education modes for people in remote areas.

During the Panchayat period also, school management committees had been responsible for mobilising resources and ensuring smooth functioning of schools. SMC members not only managed local financial support for buildings but also honorariums for the teachers appointed under *Niji Srot* (not receiving a salary from the government, but from private sources).

If any village needed a school, it had to move a proposal before the District Education Officer (DEO). A team from the DEO's office would then visit the site and submit a report on the feasibility of the proposal. If the proposal was sanctioned, the community needed to contribute towards the school building. Starting from one grade and one classroom, gradually other classes and rooms would be added (UNESCO, 1984).

## State of education, 1980–1990

Acharya (2002) found that the government opted for a more liberal policy of privatisation in the education sector in this decade. As a result, private schools emerged rapidly all over the place with higher concentrations in urban centres. The Education Act of 1980 put the responsibility of mobilising and managing financial resources for a school on the SMC. Monitoring teachers' performance also became the responsibility of the SMC (UNESCO, 1984). It was also observed that more boys were enrolled in private schools than girls, and the selection of schools was closely related to the income of the family.

After 1980, as private schools started flourishing in the country, various donors started taking an interest in funding education initiatives in Nepal. The Primary Education Project, the Basic and Primary Education Programme, Phase 1 and Phase 2 and the Secondary Education Development Project were introduced in the country with a focus on improving the quality of education with the support of funding agencies.

## State of education, 1990–2007

The return of multi-party democracy in 1990 saw an increased emphasis on education. The number of primary schools reached 14,500. In 1990, the number of lower secondary schools and secondary schools was 1,953 and 3,964, respectively (Shrestha, 1992).

'Education for All' became the slogan of the country in the changed political context and other global developments. The new government appointed a National Education Commission in 1992 to address issues of inconsistencies in the education system. This was followed by the National Education Commission in 1999 to improve the quality of education (Acharya, 2002).

In its 1992 report, the commission proposed new national goals and the restructuring of education as a 5+3+2+2 year system, for primary, lower secondary, secondary and higher secondary education.

State-run schools were never particularly good, and students coming for higher education faced difficulties in comprehension because English was the medium of instruction in higher education (Whelpton, 2005). The politicisation of the teachers along party lines after 1990, and the government's failure to meet their aspirations, eroded discipline and commitment among the teachers. Private schools expanded, as government schools could not become centres of quality learning. People who could afford private schooling for their children started sending them to private schools, as they found value in English medium education and a greater scope for opportunities in other countries as well (Acharya, 2002). Onta feels that this exodus of well-off families and their children from public schools led to the official neglect of the quality of such schools and the perpetuation of an 'education based class system' in Nepal (2000, p. 4095). Onta's conclusion, apart from highlighting the inequalities in the Nepali educational structure, casts light on the nature of the state at that time, which as an institution of service provision largely catered to elite interests.

As the Panchayat system came to an end, the vision for Nepal was also re-conceptualised with a multi-party democracy after 1990. Multi-ethnicity, multilingualism and constitutional monarchy with democracy were constitutionally accepted by the government (Hutt, 1993).

Nepal's population was 23.43 million in 2000, with a population growth rate of 2.4 per cent. However, in 2000 the total literacy rate did not exceed 30.4 per cent. The women's literacy rate was almost half of the male literacy rate. In Nepal, 698,000 children were out of school before the formal peace agreement was signed with CPN (Maoist) in 2007 (Andersen, 2007). The net enrolment ratio in 2001 was 81.1 per cent. The enrolment ratio for girls remained low at all levels, which showed a considerable gender bias in education. About 20 per cent of eligible primary school children did not go to school, and a large section of those who did either repeated a class or dropped out. Lack of teachers, poor quality of education, poverty and children engaging in labour were some of the factors that contributed to the number of children being out of school.

In the mid-1990s, education had become the political agenda of the Maoists, who demanded abolition of private schools and transformation of the government school system. Maoists forced some of the private schools to close down during the time of the People's War.

## Education during the People's War

The prevalence of social inequalities, poverty in rural areas and extreme forms of caste discrimination triggered the rise of Maoist resistance, or the People's War. The insurgency that began in 1996 resulted in an estimated 13,000 deaths (including teachers and children) and affected development activities, government budgetary allocations, the national economy and politics (Lawoti, 2010).

There have been gross regional disparities in Nepal. Facilities in terms of infrastructure, roads and electricity were better developed in urban areas but it was expensive for parents living in villages to send their children to live in towns. While the teacher-pupil ratio (TPR) in Nepal as a whole was 1:38 (in 2000), there were reports of considerable regional disparities. While the average TPR was 1:26 in Kathmandu, it was 1:46 in the Terai and 1:42 in the western region during the People's War. The retention rate up to 5th standard was only 44.4 per cent for the country (Technical Review of School Education-3, 2007).

The conflict obviously left its mark. The most glaring effect was in terms of failure to ensure uninterrupted functioning of schools within the conflict-ridden areas. Teachers were reluctant to accept postings in such areas, especially in view of reports of torture of teachers by both the Maoists and state forces. Schools were shut down when rebels wanted to put pressure on the government to release rebel cadres, or force some other concessions from the Kathmandu government. The government was criticised for stationing army and police personnel inside school compounds and exposing students to crossfires when Maoists attacked the security forces.

There were also complaints about the use of children as soldiers, informants, cooks, porters and cultural troops for the war; abduction of children for political training; arrests of minors and their detention with adult prisoners; and use of school premises for military purposes (Manchanda, 2006).

This period, however, saw some policy changes in the education system as well. One critical change during this period included the Education Act, Seventh Amendment, 2002, which made a number of provisions for addressing the key issues in the school education system in the country. Adoption of community schools as a system of education, free education in community primary schools, teacher training and teacher licensing, de-politicisation of the teaching force, regulation of private schools, free education and incentives for Dalit children were all part of this act.

Apart from the official state of Nepal and Maoists, non-state actors also played an important role in the country's educational field. International organisations such as Save the Children Norway implemented a community-based Education Information Management System (C-EMIS) to increase community involvement in all educational activities at the local level and ran the programme through the years of conflict.

In 2006, a parallel SWAp approach (sectorwide approach) was also implemented in partnership with the government with aid received from five donors – Denmark, Finland, Norway, DFID and the World Bank. At that time Nepal was classified as being 'in conflict'. A civil society inclusive approach was followed, but according to Berry, this approach was largely unsuccessful, as the government functioned in a 'top down manner' and was suspicious of the NGOs which it believed were there just to earn money (2010, p. 590). Apart from analysing education and conflict, Berry also comments on the conflict in education by citing Vaux's observation that the divide between expensive private schools where the quality of education is better and poorly run government schools where basics are lacking, is 'not conducive to resolving the conflict' (2010, p. 591).

## Administrative structure of the school system in Nepal

Nepal has a school system characterised by great heterogeneity. To look at the school system in the country without understanding its administrative system may not help one to see the complete picture. Thus, it is important to present a brief introduction of the administrative system of Nepal.

### General administrative system

On the basis of physiographic variations, Nepal is divided into five zones – High Mountain, Mountain, Hill, Siwalik and the Terai. These are divided into 14 zones and 75 districts for administrative purposes. At the next level, there are 58 municipalities. At the sub-district level, 721 Illakas have been set up, and 3,921 village development committees are responsible for the administration at the Panchayat level. Politically, there are 205 parliamentary constituencies in the country (Dhungel, 1998).

A chief district officer (CDO) is the district head, and is responsible for maintaining law and order, convergence of services, giving administrative support to other agencies and representing the government at the district level. The CDO works in close collaboration with the Superintendent of Police (SP), who is the police chief in the district.

District level officials of various departments are part of the district development team, based at the District Development Secretariat. The secretariat consists of the Departments of Education, Culture, Drinking Water and Power, Forest, Soil Conservation, Local Development, Health and Population, and Agriculture at the district level. Local development officers (LDOs) are the lead persons in these sectors at the district level (Dhungel, 1998).

## Ministry of Education and Sports/Ministry of Education

In Nepal, the Ministry of Education and Sports manages all the educational bodies and is responsible for the overall development of education and sports in the country. This ministry was first established in 1951, and is now headed by a cabinet rank minister, supported by a state minister, along with an education secretary. Different sections are headed by officials at the joint secretary level.

In 2007, the ministry was renamed the Ministry of Education (MoE). MoE formulates educational policies and plans. The ministry also looks after the implementation of educational interventions through the various institutions which come under it.

## Structure of the education system, Ministry of Education (2007)

After the ministry was renamed the Ministry of Education in 2007, the structure of school education was:

- Early Childhood Development Classes (ECDC)
- Pre-Primary, Primary and Secondary, including Lower Secondary (Middle/Upper Primary)

### *Early Childhood Development*

Introduction of a form of Early Childhood Development (ECD) dates back to 1949, when the Montessori School was established in Kathmandu. The government agreed to put the ECD programme under the Basic and Primary Education Project (BPEP) in 1991–92, and named it *Shishu Kaksha*. Expansion of the ECD intervention in

Nepal was very limited till 2001. In the changed political scenario, the National Plan of Action set an ambitious target of establishing 74,000 ECD classes between 2001 and 2015. The ECDC/pre-primary classes (*Bal Vikash*) are of one to two years duration and serve 3- to 5-year-old children.

## Primary and secondary education

Children who complete five years of age are admitted in primary schools that cater to standards 1st to 5th. After the 5th standard, children attend lower secondary schools (*Nimna Madhyamik*), which are up to the 8th standard.

The secondary level (*Madhyamik*) provides two years education for 9th and 10th standards. A national level school leaving certificate (SLC) examination is conducted at the end of standard 10. Standard 11 and 12 are considered the higher secondary level. The Higher Secondary Education Board (HSEB) supervises higher secondary schools, which are mostly under private management. During the Panchayat system (before 1990), higher secondary education (*Uccha Madhyamik*), consisting of 11th and 12th standards, was part of the university education system and not the school education system.

The National Curriculum Framework (2005) suggested a new integrated structure and suggested that Nepali formal school education will be for 12 years with two tiers – primary and secondary. The primary level will be from grade 1 to grade 8, and the secondary level will be from grade 9 to grade 12. As preparation for primary education, two years of pre-primary education (P-level) will be provided.

## Vision and national goals for education, National Curriculum Framework (2005)

Prior to the peace agreement of 2006, attempts were made to prepare a new curriculum framework in Nepal. The document took several progressive steps to modify the vision, objectives, content, teaching methods and student assessment.

### The proposed NCF 2005 vision

> The vision of school education is to develop citizens who are knowledgeable, skilful, competent, responsible, reliable, healthy, cooperative, good mannered, ethical, optimistic, nationalistic, and humanitarian, who believe in democracy, human rights, and diversity, and who have the

ability for critical thinking to face the emerging challenges of the twenty-first century in a productive manner. Such citizens will be capable to live independently, contribute to national development, and work for national and international peace and security.

## National goals of education

The national goals of education as suggested by NCF, 2005, are:

- To inculcate respect for democracy, human rights and the will to safeguard our multicultural nation.
- To produce citizens capable of creative and critical thinking.
- To produce citizens who participate in and promote the democratic process.
- To inculcate in each individual qualities like self-esteem, self-discipline, religious tolerance, humanity and civic consciousness.
- To develop human capabilities that contribute to the development of the nation.
- To develop a strong belief in social justice, social equity and gender parity such that everyone is treated equally and fairly despite her/his caste, ethnicity, disability, gender, sexuality, region of origin and age.
- To respect and celebrate sociocultural and ethnic diversity, multilingual realities and the multicultural setting of our nation.
- To enhance social unity by inculcating a deep respect for sociocultural differences and world views present in our country.
- To help each individual develop her/his identity in both national and international contexts and lead a socially harmonious life in the modern world.
- To develop social and civic responsibility to safeguard and promote the common good.
- To nurture and develop personalities and innate abilities of each individual for successful living.
- To teach thoughtful protection and wise use of Nepal's natural and cultural resources.
- To help disadvantaged citizens like minority ethnic groups, Dalits and people with disabilities to enter the mainstream.

## Education, exclusion and spade work for the People's War

Social change has always been considered a complex process, influenced by the internal and external factors which every society faces with an accelerated pace of transition at some point in its history.

Rapid changes may arise because of a natural disaster, but education is also a dominant factor contributing to revolutionary changes in a political system. The changes can occur with peaceful means or as a result of an armed conflict. For any state or society that faces an armed conflict for a decade or longer, some positive consequences result, with some painful damages. Demographic, cultural, technological, political, economic and educational factors have been recognised as key features of social change, but in the case of Nepal, issues of education emerged on the centre stage with the political strategy of the People's War. Ex-army personnel, educated youth and teachers who had exposure to the outside world and its developmental perspectives played a significant role in raising awareness about education and rights and spreading the discourse on democracy and development in the country. These long-sustained efforts in remote pockets of the country prior to 1950 and during the Panchayat system contributed in ensuring historic changes in Nepal.

People were discriminated against on the basis of geographical location; social, religious, economic identities; gender; and language. Grievances and long-pending demands of the common people were channelised by political actors. Before entering the People's War, CPN (Maoists) identified 40 issues to present before the Deuba government in February 1996 (Muni, 2004). This 40-point demand list is popularly known as the *chalish bunde maang patra* (list attached as an Annexure). CPN (Maoists) had a strong presence in the far western and central-western pockets of the country. These pockets were historically neglected and underdeveloped. A substantial chunk of migrant workers from Nepal who are working in India come from these pockets. Knowing the sentiments of the people, Maoists put a mix of issues composed of aspects of social, developmental, educational and political significance along with nationalism and the Indo-Nepal relationship into their 40-point agenda. They demanded mother tongue–based education up to high school (*ucch-madhyamic*) and equal rights for every language in the agenda. The other significant demand was providing free and scientific medical services and education to all and that education for profit should be abolished. These demands had a logical connection with the sense of denial and discrimination faced by marginalised people, especially students. Students who had graduated from schools other than English medium ones had realised that they had reduced career opportunities and upward mobility, therefore the demands for mother tongue–based education and closure of private schools (profit making education services) attracted people towards the call for revolutionary change. Nepali has thus gained prominence and protection from the government in the last five decades. Communities practicing languages other than Nepali had their own grievances and found hope that these would be addressed if they sided with the Maoists. Many scholars see language as a contentious issue in Nepal. Caddell (2007) found a link between a mother tongue–based campaign of ethnic groups with their demand for more social and political visibility and representation in Nepal.

Equal property rights for girls were demanded to address issues of gender discrimination and gender-based violence. Considering the investment factor and opportunity costs, girls' participation in education was low in Nepal even in upper caste households. Caddell (2007) observed Maoists and ethnic activists taking up school-based activities to get support from the community, the People's War was initiated by educated people and not by illiterates. Similarly, both the top leaders of CPN (Maoists), Baburam Bhattarai and Prachanda, come from high castes – Hills, Hindus. Prachanda is a graduate and was a school teacher. Baburam Bhattarai has been regarded as a scholar. He did his schooling in a missionary school before completing his doctoral research from Jawaharlal Nehru University in Delhi (Pherali, 2010).

Women's mobility in ethnic groups and other castes like Rais, Limbus, Magars, Tharus and Doms was not restricted like it was for upper caste women, but due to discriminatory social practices and limited institutional opportunities, they could not think about formal education. Women and girls emerged as a strong support base for the Maoists during the People's War. Many women and girls were part of cultural troops and some also served in the People's Liberation Army (PLA).

Social divisions on the basis of region, caste, gender and long-pending grievances towards the monarchy were used strategically by the Maoists. Stash and Hannum (2001), estimate that in 1991, almost 38 per cent of the children below 15 years of age were not enrolled in schools.

School participation in Nepal shows a strong association with caste. It has been found in many educational studies from Nepal that children from high caste households were more likely to attend and complete schooling (Stash & Hannum, 2001). High caste groups, especially Bahun-Chetris among the premier groups, were the first to get literacy skills because of their upper strata in the caste system and their necessity to be educated in order to perform their roles as priests and rulers. This initial lead in literacy helped people of high caste to be ahead of social groups in education and to enjoy high status (Seddon, 1987). Similarly, Newars who are in high concentration in the Kathmandu valley not only had more opportunities for education, business and trade with the development of the capital but they also emerged as an influential group politically. In 1979, when 79 per cent of the children of Newars were enrolled in schools, only 31 per cent of the children from low caste backgrounds were in schools. The chances of completing the primary school cycle by the enrolled children from low castes were nearly 50 per cent (Stash & Hannum, 2001). Ethnic and caste-based divisions were legalised several years back with the introduction of the National Legal Code (*Muluki Ain*) of 1854. Provisions were made under *Muluki Ain* to establish a chain of command in the country. This policy prepared the ground for justifying hierarchy and legitimising the position of the ruling class (Höfer, 1979, cited in Caddell, 2007).

In remote villages, marginalised groups, such as Dalits and Janjatis found a pragmatic approach for resolving long-pending disputes in the People's Court of the Maoists rather than struggling to get justice through a legal court, which demanded large amounts of money and time. The justice given in the People's Court was often tilted towards the supporting group, and excluded communities.

Since most of the developmental work (road, transport, health and education services, banks, etc.) was concentrated in Kathmandu valley, people from the mountains (western part) felt excluded on the basis of their geographical location; the people of the Terai experienced discrimination on the basis of language and wanted proper representation in government jobs. All the government departments, including the army and the administration, were dominated by high caste people like Bahuns, Chetris, Thakuris and Newars of the Hills. Janjatis (Tharus, Magars, Rais, Limbus, Doms, etc.) were struggling for education and equal opportunities in all aspects in the sociocultural domain. Low literacy, lack of health and educational services, unemployment and lethargic officials were the main challenges of the Janjatis. The foremost obstacle, before Dalit/Muslim groups, was caste-religious discrimination and neglect of political representation in the Panchayat system and after. Minority religious groups (Buddhists/Muslims) wanted Nepal to be a secular and not a Hindu state, so making Nepal a secular state was also included in the Maoists list of 40 demands. Other issues related to land, livelihood and untouchability were also part of the list.

As we run through the history of education in Nepal, we do not find any firm stand from the monarchs about expanding access to schooling as the state's priority. From 330 schools in 1950, the first elected government of Nepal established 1,600 schools in 1959 followed by

600 more schools by the next year. The B.P. Koirala government could not survive for long as the king introduced a new constitution banning political parties within the provisions of the Panchayat system. Political parties had to struggle for three decades, up to 1990–91, to get a democratically elected government in Nepal with a constitutional monarchy. In the absence of political parties, the king became the absolute power holder and development work could not move at a fast pace. In addition to access to schools, the quality of teachers and education attainment of the children were below satisfactory levels. Allocation of funds, printing textbooks and provisions for teachers were inadequate in government schools. So a majority of the urban and upper caste people who benefited from limited schooling facilities started sending their children to private schools. Thus private schools started expanding in Nepal and the marginalised people who could not attend schools in the 1950s, 1960s, 1970s and 1980s were left to attend poorly equipped government schools in the name of free education.

Nepal depends heavily on bilateral and multilateral donors for development. In education, donors are important stakeholders in Nepal. Bilateral donors like India and China have strategic interests in Nepal.

It is estimated that nearly 40 per cent of the education budget comes from donors. However, since the projects supported by donors are mostly supply driven, they have not been successful in meeting the basic challenges of recruiting teachers and improving infrastructure (Ministry of Education and Sports, 2007).

Even when the government said it would provide free education, this was not free, as children were asked by school managements to give monthly fees for paying a few teachers who were appointed as *Niji Srot* teachers by the management. Provision of free textbooks was only for students up to 3rd standard, and up to 5th standard for girls. Only one printing press, Janak Printing Press, was responsible for printing all the textbooks. Teachers and parents both said that getting complete sets of books on time was a major difficulty for students, teachers and parents in remote areas.

Private schools were on the rise in the 1980s and early 1990s so the children of economically better-off families started moving to private schools. Even teachers in government schools shifted their children to private/boarding schools. Socioeconomic gaps and education choices were obvious and the differences between children from private primary schools and government primary schools were similar to those who were in school and who were out of school before 1990.

Lack of sincerity, neglect of government schools, poor infrastructure, availability of fewer schools and higher education institutes contributed to people raising their voices against the monarchy and against the slow pace of development. People who worked outside Nepal and those who had gone abroad for higher education came back with a wider perspective and became catalysts for change. Dr Baburam Bhattarai is one among them, and he announced the beginning of the People's War on behalf of CPN (Maoists).

# 4 Schools
## The battleground

Children and teachers acted as the backbone of the People's War in Nepal but they also suffered a lot. Their support gave strength to political leaders to negotiate on the political front but the initial moral support to the movement became a painful experience for a large number of students and teachers. As Caddell (2007) says, she found that the schools were perceived as symbols of a highly particular construction of the state so people opposing the state machinery targeted schools, which resulted in forced closures and loss of staff and assets.

The exact number of teachers murdered during the People's War time varies from one source to another. Education Journalists' Group of Nepal estimates that 104 teachers were killed during the People's War. The number is much higher for cases reported under abduction and torture during the People's War. Education Journalists' Group of Nepal also estimates that 928 teachers were seriously affected during this period. Teachers and students became a target of both the police as well as Maoists. Out of 104 teachers, 60 were killed by Maoists and 44 by the police force. Out of the 928 affected teachers, the state was responsible for 530 teachers. Facing threats to their lives, a substantial number of teachers left their villages and schools – 203 teachers were reported as disappeared (Sharma & Khadka, 2006).

Teachers were abducted and forced to donate money regularly for the revolution, ranging from 10 to 50 per cent of their monthly salary. At least 248 teachers were arrested or abducted in the course of the nine-year conflict. In suspicion of Maoists supporters, the state arrested 185 teachers and Maoists abducted 62 others (Sharma & Khadka, 2006).

Children and teachers suffered in several ways during and after the conflict in Nepal. As structure, perspectives, policy change with the new emerged leadership in post-conflict context. Nicolai (2009) has observed that a change in political and economic perspectives could lead to a change in administration, a different language of instruction or a new model of teachers' training, and the formation of a new curriculum and changes in Nepal very much follow these lines. Caddell (2007) found schools at the centre of political discourse and campaign, as teachers were very active in changing the political system in the country. From 1970 to the *Jana Andolan* of 1990, schools and colleges became important places for protests and unrest in Nepal because of a ban on political parties under the Panchayat system till 1990.

## Sanskrit: a contentious issue during the People's War

Resistance to Sanskrit teaching in schools is one example of using issues of education to garner support from deprived communities. As mentioned earlier, Sanskrit was not only the medium of instruction but also the base for Hindu religious education, which teaches students to perform 'Karmkand'. Sanskrit had a central role in the expansion of education in Nepal till 1960. Learning Sanskrit was a professional necessity for Bahuns (Brahmins), as they had to perform religious rituals. This also gave them a head start in literacy and education. Sanskrit was the medium of instruction in schools till 1962. Then Nepali became a medium of instruction and Sanskrit got the status of a compulsory subject in schools (Whelpton, 2005). Sanskrit continued as the medium of instruction in Sanskrit *pathsaalas*.

The king ignored other languages in the country and emphasised the unification of Nepal through a common language – Nepali. Nepali helped the monarchy to establish a strong Hill identity for Nepal, ignoring the rights of other languages, such as Maithili, Tharu, Awadhi, Newari and Bhojpuri. Nepali as a medium of instruction and Sanskrit as a compulsory subject in schools worked as a disabler for children of non-Nepali-speaking groups. Nepali has been reported as the mother tongue by less than 50 per cent of the population (GoN, 2005). Sanskrit and Nepali worked as instruments to perpetuate the values of the Hindu social structure and the monarchy. As the number of schools started expanding and community members came forward to contribute to this cause, the monarchy initiated ways to get control over these institutions administratively and ideologically. In the mid-1960s, singing the national anthem in schools became compulsory (Caddell, 2007). Like other monarchies, the central theme of the national anthem was a tribute to the king.

Gradually, private English medium schools started thriving during the 1970s so Nepali was made compulsory in private primary schools in 1974. The official reason given for this was reducing tensions among children from private and state-supported schools. Many believe that the rulers were afraid of the expansion of English medium schools, as the products of these schools could later prove to be a threat to the monarchy.

After the end of the *Panchayat* system, language rights to other groups became an issue for all socio-linguistic and political groups. This came up more strongly during the People's War. Ethnic groups demanded the right to language and Maoists supported their demand. Autonomy and language rights were promised to indigenous people by the Maoists who also strongly opposed the teaching of Sanskrit in schools during the People's War (Turin, 2005). For instance, in Dang, a legal advisor to the Mahendra Sanskrit University was attacked by Maoists. He was at home during the attack and was severely injured (Sharma & Khadka, 2006).

Three types of community lower secondary and secondary schools have been functional in Nepal since 1993:

- General Education Schools
- General Sanskrit Schools (students study Nepali, mathematics, science, social studies and Sanskrit instead of art/pre-vocational education)
- Special Sanskrit Schools known as Veda Bidyashrams (with focus on veda, karamkand, rituals with subjects like Nepali, mathematics and social studies. Students do not study English and science as subjects.)

Considering the opposition from Maoists, the government made Sanskrit an optional subject in 2003. As Sanskrit lost the status of being a compulsory subject, students could select either Sanskrit or civic education as a subject in general schools.

In this respect, teachers and political activists maintain that Maoists perceived the teaching of Sanskrit as a tool to perpetuate Hindu culture and caste-based identities. Therefore they started opposing Sanskrit teaching in schools. Some of the Sanskrit teachers were murdered and a few others left their villages under fear. In Duragaon in Lamjung, Muktinath Adhikari, Maoists killed the headmaster of Panini Sanskrit High School on the school campus. He was dragged out by the Maoists, stabbed and hanged before being shot in the head. Students from the school were forced to listen to a speech in which the Maoists blamed the teacher who they said worked as a government informant, as he did not stop teaching Sanskrit and also did not collect money from other teachers to support the People's War (Watchlist, 2005).

## Education for the classes and not for the masses

The kings and the Ranas were scared of the expansion of education and other developmental work, and kept Nepal isolated for a long period of time. The first formal school, Darbar High School was established in 1883 in Kathmandu to educate the children of the ruling elites (UNESCO, 1984). But other groups could not get financial support from the government to establish their own schools. Most of the schools established by communities in the 1950s and 1960s were one-room, one-teacher schools and mostly Sanskrit schools keeping marginalised children out of them. These schools were normally up to the 2nd or 3rd standard only. Classes above the 2nd standard were attached to high schools. High schools were situated in larger towns and so they could not be accessed by children from remote villages. The other challenge before poor children were the school fees, as schools were dependent on tuition fees and community contributions (Nepal National Education Planning Commission, 1956).

Since the community was responsible for running the schools, most of the schools were established by upper caste Hindus (Bahuns, Chetris/Thakurais, Newars) because they were able to pay the fees and take on the financial burden of other expenses of schooling for their children.

In some cases, lower caste groups and Muslims also contributed financially in building schools but their representation in the education stream was low before the 1990s (Figure 4.1). In India and other Asian countries, it was found that people who were at the top of the social structure were also at the top of the education system. So it is no wonder a majority of non-educated people came from socially marginalised groups (Smith & Cheung, 1986) in South Asian countries.

With more resources and better opportunities for education, upper caste groups dominated education and other service sectors. These included Bahuns with 12.9 per cent share of the population accounting for 45 per cent of the positions in higher education in 1997, while Chhetris and Thakurais who constituted 17.6 per cent of the population occupied 21 per cent of the positions in higher education (Rana, 1998). This gave them opportunities for further investments in education. Contrary to this, the socially excluded groups struggled for enrolment and even when these groups succeeded in getting enrolled, they often failed to ensure completion of their child's primary school education.

## 68  Schools: the battleground

*Figure 4.1* Acknowledging contribution of the community in constructing a school building
Photograph by the author at Lumbini, Nepal

In 2006, at the primary level, only 3 per cent of teachers were Dalits and 2 per cent were from marginalised Janjatis. At the lower secondary level, the representation of Dalits and Janjatis was reduced further and stood at 2 per cent for Dalits and 1 per cent for Janjatis (Technical Review of School Education-3, 2007).

In a socially structured community like Nepal, interactions between upper caste and lower caste groups were limited to work-related issues in public places. The older people belonging to upper castes resisted visiting the households of lower caste people and sharing a meal with them, even after 2006. Gradually, community schools have come to be perceived by upper caste groups to be primarily for children of excluded groups, and they, therefore, prefer to send their own children to private schools.

The location of a school is also crucial; most of the schools were started in the houses or on the verandahs of the houses of landlords/ teachers, thus making accessibility difficult for small children living at a distance and for children from lower caste families. The government school at Khungai is one such school. This school started in the house of a landlord, who was a Sanskrit teacher. The school later shifted to another location with support from the community and the government.

The village structure in Nepal also has caste-based habitations, with upper castes in the centres, surrounded by hamlets of other caste groups. Some of the children of backward caste groups (Kurmis, Yadavs) got entry in schools because of their superior economic status in some pockets. In the absence of transportation, Kahars (considered a low caste) were appointed to carry children of influential people in *dolis* to the school in the 1970s.

Through community-supported and managed schools, the monarchs addressed two issues: On the one hand, children of influential rural groups got an opportunity at education, which contributed in preparing people to serve at the lower bureaucracy levels of the king and perform religious rituals. On the other hand, religion and caste-based social hierarchy aligned with the education system gave strength and sanction to the king as the head of the state and as the incarnation of God (Caddell, 2007).

The quality of education offered by the government schools was also a major issue, besides infrastructure and finance. Almost 62 per cent of schools in the Terai region were 'over crowded'. Lack of teachers' capacity and high absenteeism were other factors which contributed to the poor quality of learning (TRSE-3, 2007).

Martinelli and Almeida (cited in Upreti, 2004) argue that feelings of unfairness and injustice, suspicion, anger, emotion and mistrust result in conflict. As Maoists used feelings of injustice in educational and economic dividends, excluded communities, such as Magars, Rais, Limbus and Dalits, were the first groups to provide extensive support to the People's War.

## Reality or myth – free education in Nepal

In the 1990s, education up to the primary level became free and also a right of every child. But, in practical terms it was not free in many ways. The textbooks never reached schools in a timely manner and the full sets were also not available in the market. Textbook grants were part of the School Improvement Plan.

As mentioned earlier, there was only one printing press (Janak Press) based in Kathmandu, which had the responsibility of printing and supplying textbooks for the entire country. Parents who could afford to purchase these books could get them at the beginning of the academic session either from Bhairahawa, Butval or Kathmandu, but sometimes the books were not available in the market. During my field visits, I inquired with several shopkeepers in the weekly market in Padariya and found that all of the textbooks were not available. Interviews with teachers also confirmed this.

Headmasters did not get all of the textbooks in an academic year and they managed with old or borrowed books. Later, provisions were made for transferring cash to schools but 65 per cent of the schools did not receive textbook grants at the beginning of the academic session prior to the peace agreement (TRSE-3 2007).

---

**Box 4.1 Faulty textbook distribution system**

'Content of the textbooks which were in use till 2000 was good but the distribution system was faulty and the students did not get complete sets of textbooks in time as all the publication was done by a single press – Janak Press, Kathmandu.'

– A teacher who left his job to work with the Maoists

---

Delay in the release of funds by the department of education was also a reason for the delayed arrival of textbooks in schools. By mid-session (September), 95 per cent of students in primary schools claimed to have textbooks, though not all of the students got complete textbook sets. All the eligible students could not get textbooks because the money distributed to the schools for purchase of books was 33 per cent less than the required amount, as enrolments were higher than estimated at the central level (TRSE-3 2007).

## Teacher management: complexity and chaos

Teacher availability and recruitment was another challenge for quality learning. As many as 85 per cent of lower secondary schools did not have a subject teacher for social science and 44 per cent required an English teacher in 2006 (Technical Review of School Education-3, 2007). In 2007, the government estimated vacancies for 60,000 teachers in schools (School Sector Reform Plan, 2007).

Teachers working in schools can be classified into five groups:

- Permanent teachers
- Temporary teachers/*Niji Srot Shikshak*

- Teachers appointed under PCF (Per Child Fund)
- Support teachers/*Rahat Shikshak*
- *Bal Shikshak* for pre-primary

Around 47 per cent of primary teachers were trained and 33 per cent had in-service training. In the case of lower secondary teachers, 41 per cent were fully trained in 2006. As many as 76 per cent of teachers were working in village schools while 54 per cent of teachers were engaged in agriculture and other jobs along with teaching (Technical Review of School Education-3, 2007).

A substantial number of temporary/contractual teachers were working with the schools and getting salaries from different sources on a trimester basis. Eighty per cent of teachers were getting salaries from the central government, 3 per cent were supported by District Development Committees/Village Development Committees (DDCs/VDCs), 2 per cent were dependent on NGOs/INGOs and 13 per cent relied on schools' own sources (Technical Review of School Education-3, 2007).

*Niji Srot* teachers depended a lot on SMCs. They were appointed by SMCs while the learners paid for their salaries. Such teachers constituted around 15 per cent of the total teachers (including NGO-supported teachers). The necessity of paying a fee forced children from marginalised communities to stay out of school. The recruitment process helped SMC members to recruit their relatives as *Niji Srot* teachers. During monarchy, SMC members were nominated by district education officials of the royal government who were faithful to the monarchy. Such factors helped upper caste groups to take advantage and maintain social dominance in education at the village level.

## Textbooks and hegemony

Dependency on external donors and the challenges created by banned political parties forced the rulers to be seen as development oriented. Attempts were made to create a Nepali identity and an image of a modern state simultaneously. School curriculum and schools as a physical space became the means for disseminating a particular vision of Nepal. High caste, Kathmandu Hill and Hindu supremacy was propagated and other groups were portrayed as 'backward' through the curriculum during the Panchayat system (Pigg, 1992). Rulers tried to reclaim their authority across the country through the school system and Nepali identity. The slogan '*Ek bhasa, ek bhesh, ek dhesh*' was encouraged by political elites to get legitimacy for the identity

*Figure 4.2* Photograph of King Gyanendra and his family members in an old textbook

Source: Used with permission of the Curriculum Center, Nepal

and vision for Nepal (Caddell, 2007). During the Panchayat system, portraits of the king were displayed in all the schools and textbook content was approved by a high-level committee. The writers of textbooks were rewarded on a competitive basis, so each tried to incorporate more content related to the monarchy to win the reward. School textbooks were used to teach values of the kingdom and the system of monarchy to young children.

Before 2007, textbooks promoted a unified Nepal (one language, one nation, one culture) with dominance of the Hill, high identity and Hindu culture. In one of the exercises given in a book, children were asked to count the number of students of the following castes in their class – Bahuns, Chetris, Newars, Rais, Gurungs and Magars (*Mero Desh, Standard 5th*).

The people of the Terai expressed pain and concern over the discrimination that they claimed they were facing on the issue of identity and representation. Their claim was validated through the examination of textbooks, in which the pictures used (flowers, attire, architecture, men and women) related to the Hill area while representation of the Terai was missing.

The royal family was glorified and all the services used *Sahi* (Royal) as an adjective before the name, such as *Sahi Yatayat* (Royal Transport) and *Sahi Sena* (Royal Army). Some lessons were exclusively dedicated to the royals. In 2005, when King Gyanendra took over all power in his hand, pictures of his family were added at the beginning of the textbooks (Figure 4.2). Books were also published in the name of *Sri 5 ko Sarkar* (Royal Government of Nepal).

The Maoists ensured that the photographs and content related to the king and his family were in the districts where they dominated during the People's War. As the monarchy came to an end, the government banned all photographs and other content that mentioned or praised the monarchy (the government order is given in Annexure I).

## National anthem and hegemony

The national anthem ('Shri Maan Ghhambhir Nepali . . .') was also a contentious issue during the years of transition, as it praised only the king. Singing the national anthem and having a portrait of the king were made compulsory in schools in 1961. Prior to this, students prayed to Goddess Saraswati in schools (Onta, 1996).

The singing of the national anthem was stopped by Maoists in their areas of domination during the People's War (Mage & D'Mello, 2007). It was replaced by a new national anthem in August 2007.

## Students and teachers: supporters and sufferers

No big political movement against the state can be successful without the participation of students and teachers. A substantial number of children and adolescents actively participated during the years of transition in Nepal as well.

Youth wings of all political parties were responsible for mobilising school children, but this was more strategically done by the student wing of CPN (Maoist). Disruption of communication, transportation and schools was a part of the Maoist strategy to develop a base area and win the People's War.

A special drive was launched by Maoists during the People's War to recruit children and youth with the slogan *Ek ghar, ek jana* (one youth from every household). The families who supported the Maoist ideology sent members to work with them, while the others attended Maoist programmes under fear and faced challenges of psychosocial trauma. A large number of children, youth and families migrated to cities in India during this time. A large number of school children from the far western districts, such as Doti, Achham, Dadeldhura and Darchula, ran away to India under fear of abductions and forced recruitments. Teachers and students were often asked to be part of political rallies and protests. In an incident in Kailali, 36 teachers fled with 1,000 school children to the neighbouring district of Dhangadi. When fights between Maoists and the police force increased, children aged 9 to 10 years also left their homes in Rukum district. The Nepali organisation Community Study and Welfare Centre (CSWC) estimates that the number of internally displaced children in Nepal is as high as 100,000 to 120,000 (Watchlist, 2005).

School children in the 12–14 years age group were abducted in groups, to be oriented to the Maoist ideology (Manchanda, 2006). Students of classes 3rd and 4th and teachers were asked to walk long distances (5 to 10 kilometres) to participate in rallies and protests. They were asked to repeat slogans like '*Raj sahi murdabad*' (Monarchy Down With/Death to) and '*Hamro jeet bhav pacchi desh ma bikash auncche*' (Once we will win, development would come in the country).

All children in areas of armed conflict are entitled to protection and care under a broad range of international, regional and national instruments. Children must have economic, social and cultural rights along with the right to education, but Mottershaw (2008) correctly observes that rights are largely absent from a debate about the applicability of human rights laws in times of armed conflict. Most of the time the parties involved in conflict either hide the cases or try to justify the engagement of children in armed conflict. Throughout the People's War, children suffered, as their rights were violated in Nepal.

Key child protection articles in the UN Convention on the Rights of the Child (CRC) are Articles 9 (family separation), 10 (family reunification across borders), 11 (illicit transfer of children), 16 (right to privacy, honour and reputation) and 19 (protection from violence, injury, abuse, neglect, maltreatment or exploitation). The four Geneva Conventions, Additional Protocol and The Rome Statute of International Criminal Court also contain various international laws regarding protection of children in humanitarian crisis (OHCHR, 2015)

Disruption of schools and examination processes were a part of the Maoist strategy to get students onto the streets. Many reports confirm the abduction of students and interruptions in the functioning of schools in addition to frequent closure of schools because of strikes and calls for *bandhs*. The *Kathmandu Post* reports an incident from Rukum district where 65 students of Birendra Secondary High School were abducted. Maoists took over the school grounds for parades, drills and mass political indoctrination in February 2004.

A former Maoist fighter claimed that some of the children who were abducted stayed back and joined the People's Liberation Army (PLA). Maoist leaders, however, deny such allegations and claim that these children were not abducted for any other reason but to arrange meetings with their parents who were in Maoist camps and serving as full-time cadres.

Though Maoists have been blamed for torturing, kidnapping and murdering teachers they also ensured regularity of the teachers, non-discriminatory classroom practices, bans on drinking alcohol in some schools and an increased number of schools functioning in some pockets (Parker et al., 2012).

According to additional data provided by INSEC, the total number of abductions by Maoist forces during the conflict was more than 85,000 in which more than 10,000 were teachers (Christine).

Political induction of children and teachers often occurred in remote locations, especially in western Nepal, and many were allowed to return after a few days of induction. The time span of abduction varied on a case to case basis, but the average time for induction as decided by the Maoists was 15 days.

In 2006, the Nepali government signed a peace accord with the Maoists to end the decade-long armed struggle. More than 6,000 child soldiers had to return home. Their family members and communities were not ready to be associated with them because of perceived threats from the administration and other political groups (Kohrt, 2007).

After the peace agreement phase, students revealed that they were asked to attend rallies and demonstrations organised by Maoists in towns and district headquarters. As in many other countries, children were also used as porters to carry arms, ammunition and commodities. Some children lost their lives and others were wounded when explosive materials that they were carrying blasted. In one such incident on 18 February 2003, two students were killed while another was seriously injured during Maoist training and firing demonstrations in Prabha Secondary School in the Baglung district (*The Kathmandu Post* Watchlist, 2005).

The Informal Service Sector Centre (INSEC) estimates the deaths of 286 children till 1996 because of armed conflict and bomb blasts. Of these 85 were girls. Further, 161 children were killed by government forces and 121 by Maoists (Watchlist, 2005).

> The Parties to the conflict shall take all feasible measures in order that children who have not attained the age of fifteen years do not take a direct part in hostilities and, in particular, they shall refrain from recruiting them into their armed forces.
> (Article 77(2), Additional Protocol I to the Geneva Conventions)

Recruitment and use of children under the age of 15 is prohibited by the Convention on the Rights of the Child and the Additional Protocols to the Geneva Convention. The Rome Statute of the International Criminal Court (ICC) echoes this stance. The Convention on the Rights of the Child's Optional Protocol on the Involvement of Children in Armed Conflict (2000) requires state parties to increase to 18 years the minimum age for compulsory recruitment and for direct participation in hostilities and prohibits non-state armed groups under any circumstances from recruiting or using children under 18 years. Children as well as all other detainees must be treated humanely, including an absolute ban on torture and cruel, inhuman and degrading treatment (OSRSG-CAAC, 2009).

Maoist groups forcefully recruited and used children, both in support roles and for combat in the People's War. Children did not have a choice; they were arbitrarily detained, tortured for their perceived or actual association with the government and used as human shields.

> **Box 4.2 Forced recruitments**
>
> Even by conservative estimates, 7,000 to 10,000 children were abducted during the conflict. Schools were used extensively to recruit children and organise 'cultural' events by Maoists and government forces who also used these buildings as barracks. Cases of forced recruitments of children have been reported by some and the Watchlist report (2005) says that the number of children under 18 years of age with the Maoists was around 30 per cent of their total strength.
>
> **'Come with us, or do you want to die?'**
>
> Henang had no choice when he was kidnapped at the age of 13 by Maoist guerrillas in Nepal. 'It was purely chance that it was me. When the Maoists came to our school and asked the way to the nearest village, terrified pupils ran in all directions. A guerrilla soldier pointed his pistol at me and threatened to kill me if I didn't go with them,' he says.
>
> When Henang finally escaped after nine months, he was covered with marks and scars from beatings. He was terrified of his commander. 'I tried many times to get away. Every time I was caught and beaten by the commander. He always watched me, threatened me and hit me. I hated him,' he adds. That is why Henang even thought of killing the commander one evening when the opportunity came.
>
> Henang was taken into custody by the army, who immediately pressured him to tell them which villages had cooperated with the guerrillas and the villagers were punished. Now Henang cannot go home because he is seen as an informer and a traitor.
>
> Source: Save the Children (2007)

Fifteen-year-old Santosh Biswokarma was allegedly kidnapped, tortured and finally killed by Maoists in Dahankuta district. Maoists found him guilty of robbery and rape (Watchlist, 2005). A group of three girls aged between 15 and 16 years were killed by plain clothes police personnel while returning from school. They were coming back after performing a cultural event, probably organised by Maoists (*Kathmandu Post*, 2004).

Some young people joined the police/army, while others opted for the PLA of the Maoists as a career option. Other than a desire to change the political system, coming under the influence of the ideology and because of unemployment, fears of survival in a conflict situation and poverty were some of the reasons that motivated children and youth to join the PLA and contribute towards the success of the People's War.

Nearly 40,000 people migrated from villages and had not returned before the Comprehensive Peace Agreement of 2006 (CWIN, 2009). A student of class 5th narrates his story, 'The insurgents ordered me to carry a heavy load of stones. They treated me as the son of their enemy. When my parents were threatened to death, we left Jhajarkot and came to this area' (Jnawali et al., 2006, p. 32).

Maoists opposed the functioning of private schools in general. Many schools were forced to give money while some were attacked and bombed. The Global IDP project estimates that around 700 private schools were shut down during the People's War. Most of these schools were in Gorkha, Baglung, Syangia, Tanahu, Dang and Surkhet districts (Watchlist, 2005).

Some of the children from economically well-off families were sent to boarding schools in India. Some took admission in government schools and others entered into the workforce and moved to cities to work. Functional government schools became overcrowded as new students moved to safer places, so schools particularly in Saptari, Sunsari and Udaypur districts became overcrowded. Students had to be placed outside classrooms, as all of them could not be accommodated in a moderate-sized classroom. In Bajura district, the higher secondary school in Martadi was asked to vacate its premises by the police in 2002. The teachers decided to move the school to a falling down hospital building. The presence of security personnel outside schools and the fear of attacks by the Maoists also contributed to displacement and migration of students. Poorly equipped classrooms, lack of textbooks and learning materials, and teachers working under pressure stymied learning.

Recruitment exposes children to a number of extreme risks, such as death, physical injuries, psychological damage and sexual abuse. Sexual violence and exploitation are chronic risks for both girls and boys in conflict situations. Rape and other forms of sexual violence against children are serious violations of international human rights laws. In 2009, the Security Council (Resolution 1882), added sexual violence against children as an additional trigger for listing parties to conflict in the Secretary General's Annual Report on Children and Armed Conflict (OSRSG-CAAC, 2009).

The obligation of a humane treatment under Common Article 3 of the Geneva Conventions implicitly prohibits rape or any other sexual violence, be it against adults or children. ICC's Rome Statute states that rape, sexual slavery, enforced prostitution or 'other forms of sexual violence of comparable gravity' may constitute war crimes and crimes against humanity (OSRSG-CAAC, 2009).

Some children facing security and livelihood challenges get trapped in trafficking nets. During the People's War, trafficking of children saw an increase in Nepal. Laczo (2003) reveals that roughly 600,000 girls and young women were 'missing' from Nepal. Many of them had been trafficked and forced to work as sex workers in big cities in India. People also maintain that other than sending children to India for domestic help, carpet weaving and sex trade, children were also sent to Gulf countries and to some European countries during the People's War.

The role played by the teachers was significant in ensuring many changes in Nepal. When the political movement started in the 1990s, teachers played an active role in mobilising people and generating awareness about their rights. Some political activists, who were earlier teachers by profession, shared that teachers were in a position to articulate the grievances of the people and had an understanding of state transformation processes. Many of them had left their jobs and became full-time workers of political parties like CPN (Maoist), Nepali Congress and Communist Party of Nepal (Unified Marxist Leninist). Some went underground during the People's War. As many as 141 teachers were killed by Maoists and by the state's armed forces (IRIN News, 2006). Many teachers were kidnapped and tortured as they resisted the Maoists and state forces. In Parsa district, Birendra Yadav, a school teacher in the Sauraha Primary School was shot dead by some unknown persons during the People's War. Basnet (2005) has captured a few stories of teachers who were kidnapped and killed as they were not 'cooperating' with the People's War.

Harsa Subedi of Deependra Secondary School in Bhojpur district was killed when he was on his way to Tribhuvannagar Municipality. Gokharan Aryal of Makawanpur was also murdered by rebels (Sharma and Khadka, 2006).

In conflicted democracies, the human rights of people are violated by the group who holds state power and the group who is fighting to remove the state power. Both the groups describe their acts as legitimate in the larger interest of the masses (Gross, O., & Ni Aolain, F., 2006).

I met a teacher in Sindhupolchowk district in 2008, who had been kidnapped twice but who did not admit to this in his meeting with me because of fear. Later during a community meeting in the evening, the informants told me that he had been kidnapped.

Teacher Narjit Basnet was abducted by Maoists for not obeying their diktats; they also chopped off his left hand not only as a punishment for not obeying them but also to generate fear among the teachers so that they could seek more support from them. This inhuman act did not stop Basnet from performing his duties as a teacher. He still manages to teach children in a community school (IRIN News, 2006).

Teachers were also pressurised to motivate children and bring them to political rallies. Those who opted to maintain a neutral stance were forced by Maoists to give financial contributions on a monthly basis. The amount for this ranged between 5 and 50 per cent of their salaries. A reasonable number of teachers offered voluntary support to Maoists. The Education Journalists' Group of Nepal has collected cases of teachers who were abducted, kidnapped, tortured and murdered during the People's War. The teachers in Karnali Higher Secondary School in Kailali district were forced to donate 5 per cent of their salaries to the rebels. Saying no to donations had its own repercussions. Lal Bahadur Shahi dared to refuse the demand of donations by Maoists. He was serving in Bhairab Nath Lower Secondary School, Bajura, when he was kidnapped for not adhering to the Maoists' demand. The Gandak Bureau of Maoists western region command circulated a note in Palpa district in which teachers were asked to donate 12 days of their monthly salaries to make the revolution a success (Sharma & Khadka, 2006).

Some teachers who were suspected as Maoists supporters became the target of security forces. In Nuwakot, a teacher in the Siddhi Ganesh Secondary School was arrested by security personnel dressed in plain clothes. Thirteen school teachers in Balhit Secondary School in Tansen were beaten up by security forces, and in protest all schools in the area were closed for a few days.

Many teachers became victims of state atrocities as well. Like Hari Prasad Bhattarai, Sibhalaya, a teacher in the Chisapani Higher Secondary School in Dambarakhu, was killed with his two relatives, Dak Mani Koirala and Durga Prasad Koirala. Both the youths were active in student politics and were affiliated with the Nepal Students Union. It is said that security forces were behind the killings.

Balman Baraily, a 28-year-old teacher in Kalika School in Morang, was returning home from school when he was arrested by plain clothes personnel. Later on, he was found dead near another Devkota Primary School (Sharma & Khadka, 2006).

---

**Box 4.3 Maoists had more control over schools than the government**

Source of revenue

Schools were a major source of revenue for the Maoists. Monthly 'contributions' was imposed on teachers' salaries – 10 per cent tax on the salary was an average amount of 'donation' in Terai. We had no option as Maoists had more control over the schools than the government in many parts of the country.

– A teacher in Lumbini

Source: Interaction with the author

---

Maoist leaders accept that teachers gave financial contributions to make the People's War a success. A Maoist leader has stated that, 'Even within Maoists, some people were *khaowadi* (opportunists), and not real *maowadi* (Maoist) and now we are aware of this.'

Those who wanted to remain neutral sent other members of their families to demonstrations organised by political groups, especially the Maoists. Goffman (cited in Miller & Dingwall, 1997, p. 8) calls this 'Felicity's Condition', that is, we act in such a way so as not to disconfirm the assumption of our sanity by those around us. Some teachers reported that they were also asked to write slogans on the walls of their schools, for which the content was given by political cadres.

In areas with Maoist influence, teachers who had disagreements with local Maoists were forced to leave the place, and they lived with regular threats. A large number of teachers were kidnapped for a few days but few dared to share their stories. The Education Journalists' Group of Nepal has documented a detailed list of teachers who were abducted and attacked during the People's War.

In Dohalaka district, Udhav Siwakoti, a teacher in Kalinag Secondary School was murdered after being abducted. Two more teachers, Tilak K.C. and Dalkaji Yogi, were abducted by Maoists for a few days. In Ramecchap district, Krishna Gopal Shrestha was in his class in Yashma Secondary School when the rebels dragged him outside the classroom and beat him so badly that they broke his leg. They left him crying before the terrified school children. One more teacher in Ramecchap district, Som Bhadur Mahat, was abducted. When he tried to flee from captivity, the Maoists caught him and kept him in a labour camp.

Security forces arrested Chakra Bahadur Katuwal, the headmaster of Kuhibhir Secondary School in Okhaldhunga. He has still not returned and no one knows his location.

> **Box 4.4 Teaching to car washing: story of displacement**
>
> During 2001, Mahesh (not his real name) worked as a volunteer teacher in a primary school in his village in Bajura district. He was abducted and held for 10 days by the Maoists and was asked to join the PLA, which he refused to do in front of a Politburo. He was given an alternative of making a contribution of 50,000/NC for the People's War, which also he could not do. During 2002, his brother-in-law (who was in RNA) came to meet his family members. After staying there for the night, he went back in the morning. Mahesh went to see him off at the public transport. While coming back, Mahesh was stopped by Maoists. They started beating him with iron rods and belts. They accused Mahesh of being an informer for RNA. Due to the beating, Mahesh lost consciousness. The Maoists left the wounded and unconscious Mahesh in the forest and fled.
>
> As Mahesh did not return home, his family members started searching for him. His mother found him, and then the family members took him to a doctor in Mahendra Nagar. All the male members left home immediately. In Mahesh's absence, his wife (who had a three-month-old baby) was detained by Maoists for 27 days. RNA personnel visited the family during the day, as they suspected Mahesh's family to be Maoist supporters; the Maoists came at night suspecting the family's association with RNA. In such a fearful environment, the remaining members of the family also left home one night, leaving behind the house, food, livestock and other belongings.
>
> Mahesh did not return to his village from the hospital. Instead, he went to Delhi with the ambition of taking a computer course,

while working part time. He asked his wife and children to stay with his in-laws in Mahendra Nagar. He started working in a warehouse in Lajpat Nagar, Delhi. He thought he would go back to his village soon and would start teaching in the school for which his father had donated the land. After a gap of seven years (in 2009), he dared to go back to explore whether he could get his job back. He stayed there for more than a year, but nothing concrete happened.

His elder daughter, who was then 12 years old, fell and broke her leg. Mahesh spent around 60,000 (Nepali rupees), but she did not recover. He returned to Delhi in the last quarter of 2010 with his wife and two daughters. His elder daughter is still being treated at AIIMS.

Mahesh washes cars in the morning and works in a department store during the day. His other daughter is in Nepal with his in-laws. Every month he sends some money there.

Mahesh's head still has scars. He still gets frightened remembering the day he was attacked. He has a dream to establish a good school in his village. He wishes to serve his own community in the future.

Source: Interaction with the author

As mentioned earlier, other than the regular demand of *Chanda* (monetary contributions), Maoists also asked teachers to participate in demonstrations, make arrangements for stay and rations for its cadres and send students for rallies. In Terathum, school teacher Prem Hangshrod was kidnapped along with his 15-year-old son. This teacher in Sandhu Secondary School and his son came back home after paying a 'donation' of Rs 50,000 (Sharma & Khadka, 2006).

Maoists, however, also had a support base among the teachers, and some teachers who were associated with the Maoists left their jobs and went underground to work as full-timers. Now, many of them are working as political activists with CPN (Maoist).

Tejendra J. Pherali (2011) found Maoist supporters among teachers. He observed that Maoists were enjoying the moral support of a considerable number of school teachers and state employees for continuing the People's War.

Teachers' affiliations with political parties emerged as a serious issue. Teachers did not talk to each other on political issues, as they did not trust each other in a chaotic political situation. A leader of Nepali Congress expressed his anger in these words: 'Teachers, who have been associated with the Maoists, are still (post Peace Agreement and election of 2008) doing party work instead of teaching children in schools.'

## Attacks on schools

UNESCO defines attacks on education as 'any intentional threat or use of force directed against students, teachers and education institutions, carried out for political, military, ideological, sectarian, ethnic, religious or criminal reasons' (International Committee of the Red Cross, 2010).

> The parties to the conflict shall at all times distinguish between the civilian population and combatants and between civilian objects and military objectives and accordingly shall direct their operations only against military objectives.
> (Article 48, Additional Protocol I, Geneva Conventions)

Deliberately targeting schools or hospitals in the absence of military necessity is prohibited under the general legal principle of distinction, meaning that civilian objects must be distinguished from military objects and protected against the consequences of military operations. This is a customary norm of international law applicable to all parties to conflict in all conflict situations.

Schools and hospitals are civilian institutions that often provide shelter and protection and cater to the needs of children during conflict. Attacks against schools or hospitals are, in principle, infringements of well-established international humanitarian law and may constitute war crimes and crimes against humanity. The Convention on the Rights of the Child recognises the paramount importance of children's right to education and right to health. The targeting and destruction of schools or hospitals obviously constitutes an obstacle to fulfilling these rights.

During the People's War in Nepal, the functioning of schools was seriously affected by the conflict and they were disproportionally targeted by all the parties. Widespread military use and the targeting of teachers and attacks on schools and hospitals by the parties involved in the People's War severely disrupted children's access to education services in Nepal.

O'Malley (2010) lists the following factors which are responsible for attacks on schools and hospitals:

> Parties may seek to undermine the authority of the state, to take revenge, to show strength, to drive out intellectuals, to recruit, to terrorise, to degrade infrastructure, to abduct for ransom and/or to occupy premises.

In Nepal, most of these reasons existed, as schools provided support for the People's War for change but now they are struggling to move on with increased awareness and painful experiences during the period of the war and after.

Maoists opposed private boarding schools, as they were not in favour of a two-tier school system (private and government) in the country. Private schools were forced to give 'donations' for the People's War. They locked many private schools and succeeded in shutting some down forever in districts in eastern Nepal (Gautam, 2004). In 2004, St. Joseph's School in Gorkha district was attacked and some computers broken. Similarly, buses of Modern Indian School in Kathmandu were set on fire by the Maoists on 9 June 2004. The computers in the schools were damaged.

The armed forces raided a meeting of Maoists in Bidya Mandir Higher Secondary School in Binayak village in Accham district using a helicopter. Six people died in the firing and some children were injured. Following all these incidents, some more schools in the area were closed down. Prior to this, even in 2002, firing had taken place between Maoists and the police during the school hours in Mahabir High School in Chainpur in Sirha district. The school was closed for more than a week and when it reopened not all of the children came back initially.

Wessel and Hirtum (2013) elaborate on the reasons why armed forces and Maoists used schools in Nepal. They say that schools are the most spacious places in most of the villages. The buildings are suitable for shelter and storage. The playgrounds attached to schools are appropriate to hold rallies, recruitment drives, meetings and cultural events.

Hence, schools were used as barracks by both the warring groups. Classes were often suspended by the armed groups as they took shelter in the premises and organised militia training. In some schools, Maoists engaged students to make safety arrangements so that they could stop the police from coming in. *Kantipur* (2004) reported that Maoists were digging 200 metres long and 3 metres deep in many schools in Accham.

Child Workers in Nepal (CWIN, 2009) estimates that nearly 3,000 schools were closed between January and October 2005 due to strikes called by the Maoists' students union. INSEC estimates that more than 75 schools and 13 education offices were attacked and ransacked by Maoists between 2002 and 2006.

## Children in war zones

Civilians face victimisation from one or both of the warring parties in insurgency. Non-participation can be a greater risk than participation (Eck, 2010). Therefore, whatever be the case, children are perhaps the worst affected group in any society in conflict. In Sirha, 13-year-old Sita Kumari lost her life when Maoists threw a bomb on a nearby police station. In Nepal, children were placed in high risk zones by the Maoists. Yam Bahadur Gurung, a ninth grader in Iritar Secondary School in Ilam, was hit by a bullet that killed him.

One more innocent girl, 12-year-old Sona Singh, was killed when she was caught in a crossfire (Sharma & Khadka, 2006).

---

### Box 4.5 Students as targets

During the years of insurgency, 378 students were arrested and 5,716 students were abducted (Thapa & Koirala, 2012).

---

The argument given by Maoist leaders is that during the People's War, common people, including children, came to fight with suppressed forces. Children were frontline fighters and part of mass attacks on police posts. In the 10-year-long People's War, nearly 475 children died, of which 205 were girls (CWIN, 2009).

Orientation and recruitment of children in PLA was part of the Maoists' strategy as well.

---

### Box 4.6 Santosh*

Santosh (who served in PLA and never attended any school) has been associated with Maoists for the last seven years and has stayed at the PLA's camp for 18 months. He was the one who motivated some other friends to join PLA. People from the area think that Santosh is a 'hard core/dreaded Maoist'.

The police visited his house and tried to pressure his family members. He then warned the police personnel that they also had families who could be killed.

He argued that if the government had agreed to fulfil the 40-point demand, then there would not have been any 'Janyudh'. The working relationship has changed now because every youth of Nepal has 'Chetna' about injustice as well as potential.

Pointing at his guerrilla friends, Santosh said that they regretted not having been properly educated. With education, they would have served the community as doctors, planners or media personnel. In place of carrying books and pens, they had to carry guns. He said that they even cried sometimes and that they missed being with their parents.

Santosh further said that in Maoist camps there were punishments for mistakes, such as cleaning vessels and stone crushing. Some went in the camp to enjoy power but faced a hard life; some went to get guns, so that they could wield power; but in some cases, people were kept forcefully in the camps so as to save their lives from the police force. It was very difficult to get leave (even if someone was getting married in the family or someone in the family had passed away) because there was always the fear of an attack by the police force, so they came three or four days after such an occasion in a group and such meetings were only for a few hours. They had nicknames for everybody, for example, Chotu, Suraj, Pucche, Raj, Attack and so on.

Code words, such as the following, were used during attacks:

| Real Word | Code Word |
| --- | --- |
| Grenade | Dunga |
| Bullet | Chilli (Khurasani) |
| Open Fire | Pilli-Pilli |
| Doctor | Mama |
| Mine | Patthar |
| Retreat | Akash |

Santosh is now looking for a job but nobody is ready to hire him because of his former political linkages.

*Name changed on request.

Source: Interviewed by the author.

## School: strategic place for all

Historically, in Nepal, schools were established by the community, and after school hours, they were used as community spaces. In the absence of any other facility under collective ownership at the village level, schools were traditionally used in many ways by many actors. Before the 1990s, school playgrounds and verandahs were used by the king's local officials to conduct meetings with villagers. Subsequently, they were used by political parties and community members for meetings and social gatherings.

As the People's War intensified, school buildings were the safest places for security forces as well as Maoists and they used the school spaces to conduct meetings, to recruit new cadres and to hide out and store arms and ammunition. Maoists also performed cultural events in schools to diffuse allegations against them and to glorify their acts of violence.

In some cases, exchange of fire took place between the Maoists and the police in school campuses resulting in injuries and even in the deaths of students and teachers (Basnet, 2005). On 13 October 2003, security forces entered Shree Sharada High Secondary School in Mudbhara ward in Dhoti district where Maoists were having a cultural event. Teachers as well as students were forced to attend the event. Security forces started firing and a few Maoists tried to hide behind students, using them as shields. Four students were killed, five were injured and six Maoists were gunned down.

There have also been reports that mines and other explosive devices were placed in and around school buildings and playgrounds.

## Potential child soldiers: out-of-school children

Other than the historical reason of poor access to schools, conflict made schooling even more challenging. The survival rate of students up to class 5th was less than 50 per cent, and considering political volatility and field experiences, the number of out-of-school children would have been even more. It was estimated that 698,000 children in the 6–14 year age group were out of school in Nepal before the peace agreement of 2006 (Andersen, 2007).

The closure of schools for days kept children out of school. In some districts in the Terai region, schools were shut down for months. Chances of 'out-of-school' children joining armed groups has been high in all the countries under conflict. This was the case with Nepal as well. A sizeable number of former child soldiers in Nepal were dropouts.

### Story of a school dropout who joined PLA

The conflict and transition changed Nepal as a state. This change affected each Nepali citizen, but young individuals who chose the path of rebellion and picked up weapons had a difficult life during the transition. At an age when children are supposed to be in schools, they were in Maoist camps as young guerrillas. A case of a guerrilla is presented here so that the involvement of young people in the Maoist movement can be understood better.

After completing 7th standard, Shubash migrated to Mumbai, India, so that he could work and earn some money. He was only 12 years old then. He worked as a helper and as a tailor in Mumbai for four years and then returned to his native village in Nepal where he joined the Maoists. He took part in many guerrilla attacks on behalf of the Maoists and spent almost 18 months in a PLA camp during the People's War in 2005. Regarding joining PLA, he says,

> I saw some people with arms in the local market forcing vendors to shut down the shops and then asked 'why do you force people to close down the market?' The group shared its view on the exploitative nature of the state as well as the landlords and later on gave some literature to read which included reading material and books such as *Chamkelo Taro, Itihasik Dastaveze* by Baburam Bhattarai, Sainya Prasikshan, Sainya Akhil Vigyan and books written by Maxim Gorki.

Shubash was influenced by the discussion and literature. He decided to join PLA when he was 16. He said, '*Laam baddh ho gya*' (I got associated). Shubash's grandfather also shared stories of exploitative 'Choudhary' (local landlords) and their *julm* (exploitation/misdeed) of poor people, including his family. This factor also influenced his decision to join the PLA.

He was kept in Krishna Singh Smriti Brigade, Battalion No. 3, for a week so that he could attend training classes and take part in the physical training. A week later, he appeared for the test. He successfully passed the test and was sent to the 4th Battalion at PLA headquarters, Arun Khola.

Under high security, Shubash regularly attended classes with some other recruits for two months. The day-long sessions were divided between classroom teaching and hands-on experience of using guns and explosives. The theory part of the training covered a range of subjects including *vaigyanik samyavad* (scientific communism), *rajniti sastra* (political science) and *darshan sastra* (philosophy). The teachers were quite good and equal to the rank of commanders in PLA.

Shubash took part in six attacks: 'Many times, we went in a group of 6,000–7,000 people,' he says. The work division was very rational, so strategies were drafted by the seniors based on the information provided by women informants. All the fighters had to attend preparatory sessions, where code words were given to them. Groups were formed with specific tasks. One 'resource' group was responsible for supplies of arms and ammunition, another group was first assault, which was equipped with light machine guns (LMGs); the second assault team was responsible for defence and there was also a doctor's group for medical assistance. Before the attack, land mines were placed by the women's group behind the target (place or building). So, during the attack, if the enemy tried to escape, the land mines would make the task futile. There were many women in the first assault also. Most women were from western Nepal and could not attend schools for a variety of reasons. Some of the women had been raped and tortured, and that had led them to join PLA. The Royal Nepal Army was the prime enemy for PLA. Recalling his participation in attacks, Shubash said that Mankamna, Palpa, Gorai and Kapilvastu were some of the memorable attacks in which he took part. He further explained that a splendid event was organised before departure for an attack. In such an event, people got delicious food. They lunched together. The environment of such gatherings was emotional. The fighters felt like *baratis* (members of a marriage party). They were uncertain about their safe return.

Some of his friends were killed (he called it *Sahadat*) in front of him during the attacks. They left their friends behind and moved ahead. For them, it was very depressing to see their friends, with whom they had lunched only a few hours ago, lying in pools of blood. At the same time, it gave them the courage to take revenge.

Everybody had to return to a report-back point to meet others. In some cases, some of their friends came back after three or four days and then there was a grand welcome celebrating the 'homecoming' of 'lost' friends.

When a guerrilla fell in love with someone in the camp, he had to write an application to the commander and then a face-to-face interaction was organised. After an observation period of 6 to 12 months, if both partners agreed to marriage, then a 'Marxist marriage' with a garland and *sindoor* was arranged for them. They celebrated such occasions.

Shubash added that in the beginning some minor children were also involved (aged 13 to 15 years). Four brigades made up one division.

One brigade consisted of 2,000 to 2,500 personnel. Food was cooked by a group of 50 to 100 people. Most of the time, they were dependent on 'chow-chow'. Sometimes, they got food with help from the villagers. He claimed that the villagers were very cooperative and supported them. They stayed in the jungles but made their own houses as well. After the Comprehensive Peace Agreement, the quality of food improved. They had classes for illiterates in the barracks. They constructed roads for the villagers and connected villages with electricity. They also worked in the villagers' farms.

Regarding Maoist strategies, Shubash said that they were instructed by the leaders to stop three things: communication, schools and transportation. Students being the major force of any political process were taken for a *juloos* (procession). Large student gatherings were used to pressure the state.

He added that after the Comprehensive Peace Agreement of 2006, they got regular rations from the government. He claimed that the reason for the conflict was the underdevelopment of Nepal. The education system did not promote a scientific attitude. If anybody like Baburam Bhattarai wanted to do something, he was not allowed to do that; political parties (Nepali Congress) were guided by foreign players. He expressed displeasure at the fact that despite having a huge potential for generating electricity, Nepal did not use this for its own people. He claims that currently Nepal is producing only 6,000 megawatts of electricity and selling most of it to India. If Nepal would produce 76,000 megawatts of electricity then every youth of Nepal could have his own motor bike. Nepal has adequate natural resources like coal and gas, but it is sold to other countries only to be purchased back at a higher price.

He complained:

> Our education system does not train us or equip us with skills. We need good schools. In the present situation, 75 per cent of students are unable to get quality education. The remaining 25 per cent from rich families are getting quality education in private schools but they will fly away.

In 1996, when Janyaudh was announced by the Maoists, Dil Bhadur Ramtel, a 14-year-old student, was the first 'martyr' who was gunned down by the Royal Nepal Army.

Some party workers started 'dadagiri' in the name of the party and collected 'contributions' while the party never asked for forced contributions. These forced contributions not only reduced the support base of the Maoists in the Madhesi population but also resulted in a loss of support for guerrillas.

Shubash spent two years in a camp and sometimes felt bad that he could not see his family members. Once his group encountered a group of six military personnel in Palpa and the military personnel surrendered before them. In spite of their surrendering, Shubash's group had to shoot them all, as those were the orders of the superiors. This fills him with guilt. But he still carries PLA's badge in his wallet and feels proud that he can operate sophisticated weapons. He said that he hopes that the Maoists win the Constituent Assembly elections with support from the oppressed (*utpidit*) sections of society.

## Overcrowded classrooms

After the People's War, teachers highlighted the fact that parents and SMCs were more watchful in the hills and valleys about teachers' availability in schools and their punctuality, in comparison to the Terai region. It was also found during classroom observations that small children did not have any systematic engagement with teachers.

Teachers' organisations have increased in number and more than 12 teachers associations are actively working in the post-conflict phase. Raising a concern on poor quality of education and politicised teachers, a professor at Tribhuvan University states 'Teachers are divided along party lines in Nepal. They are more politicians than teachers as their bosses are political leaders, not teachers and this is the major concern of education in Nepal.'

When the children of upper caste groups moved to private schools, parents from marginalised communities did not find poor quality education useful. Parents often asked children, especially girls, to stay back at home during the harvest season. I met two small girls (enrolled in standard 2) who were staying back to manage a '*paan*' shop, as their parents worked in the fields. It could be said that with poor quality education, enrolment as well as chances of completing primary education seem a challenge, particularly in the case of girls and children of marginalised communities, even after a change of guard.

## Parallel government

Rukum, Rolpa, Jajarkot and Salyan were some of the districts in the western part of Nepal with a strong presence of Maoists, and parallel governments were functional here during the People's War (Manchanda, 2006). Government offices, banks, police posts and schools were attacked and captured (Varma, 2005) by Maoists right from the beginning of the revolutionary movement. Educational programmes based on the state curriculum could not be implemented in the Maoist strongholds.

Maoists introduced their own curriculum up to the 3rd standard (*Education vs education*, 2005) with focus on their ideology and ideologues.

## Suspension of funds

Conflict not only destroys school buildings, furniture and so on, but also the hopes and ambitions of a whole generation of children (UNESCO, 2011), and to rebuild all these, funding is a crucial factor for economically weak countries.

As Nepal has been heavily dependent on international aid for social development initiatives, reduced international investment in education further increased its challenges. Funds from developmental projects got diverted and some welfare initiatives were suspended in Nepal. At a time when schools needed more money, the then government diverted funds from the social sector to defence and the police. India supplies most of the arms and ammunition to Nepal, but in 2003, Nepal approached the United States to purchase automatic rifles and machine guns to be in command of the Maoists uprising (Small Arms Survey, 2003).

Donors do not prefer aid to conflict affected countries so the European Commission suspended an education aid of US $30 million to Nepal. The money was to support the Education for All efforts in the country between 2004 and 2009 (Bikash, L., 2005).

The suspension and diversion of funds from the education sector made children more vulnerable, as incentives, such as scholarships and free textbooks, were not given to tens of thousands of children. A majority of the children who could have benefited with this support were from the marginalised groups.

## Recruitment of children

Former Maoist fighters accept that the recruitment of young children was a part of the Maoist strategy. They also narrate the preparation process before a mass attack, especially on police posts and the code words used to differentiate between 'own people' and 'enemies'.

Housden points out that child participation in the Maoist insurgency can be explained by several 'push' and 'pull' factors. The most commonly cited push factor is extreme poverty. Poor economic conditions and consequent lack of opportunities in many districts meant that the basic needs of many children were not met. Antipathy towards the state was exacerbated by structural discrimination endemic in many Nepali rural communities, particularly towards girls, marginalised ethnic minorities and lower caste, Dalit children. Most children who were recruited by CPN (Maoist) came from far and mid-western districts, such as Rolpa, Rukum and Jarjakot, where anti-state sentiments and underdevelopment were especially pernicious. Brooding intergenerational conflict was also a prominent push factor as children associated with armed forces and groups (CAAFAGs), who tended to be adolescents aged between 14 to 16 years, were typically frustrated with the elder generations since they were perceived as an obstacle to greater life opportunities.

However, the CPN (Maoist) was so successful in recruiting children because it implemented a strategy that tapped into these existing grievances. For instance, CPN-M organised cultural programmes of singing and dancing that included strong messages of its political ideology, which were extremely popular with children. Recruits were also promised wages, which often exceeded their average incomes. Although greater economic opportunities informed the decisions of many youths to join the insurgency, it was the status and sense of empowerment that one gained by joining the Maoists that was particularly attractive. In particular, the nature of the Maoist ideology rooted in equality and egalitarianism struck a chord with girls, lower castes and Dalits as well as other ethnic minorities who had historically been marginalised by the state. Other pull factors included peer pressure – becoming a Maoist became a cool thing to do – family involvement with the party and as the conflict progressed, revenge. Many villages experienced brutal, heavy-handed state operations. If one's father was killed or mother or sister was raped by the (Royal) Nepali Army, both of which were common incidents during the war, then motivation for joining the Maoists was bound to increase.

However, it would be a gross misrepresentation to argue that the Maoists did not force children into their ranks: fear and physical coercion were central tools for bolstering child participation. Although children enjoyed the cultural and entertainment meetings, many were also forced to attend them. Moreover, significant numbers of children were abducted from villages and were subsequently forced into Maoist ranks. The CPN-M implemented a 'One Family, One Child' policy whereby every family in a village had to supply a cadre to its forces, which invariably led to harsh and repressive reactions on those children and their families who refused the CPN-M. Nevertheless, one of the most interesting aspects of the Maoist recruitment of children, especially in comparison to conflicts in Sierra Leone or the Democratic Republic of Congo, was the relatively low levels of 'forced participation' in active insurgency.

Housden further explains that while most children were given some form of military training once they joined the Maoists, they tended to fulfil non-military roles in the insurgency on a part-time basis. Such roles included being messengers, spies or cooks and were usually performed by recruits aged between 10 and 16 years.

Children also formed part of the state's security forces although to a much a lesser extent. Captured Maoist children formed the bulk of the state's child forces. Child captives were forced to accompany reconnaissance missions and provide sensitive information about the homes and bases of senior Maoist military personnel. In some cases children lied about their age to get into the (Royal) Nepal Army for it provided a lucrative source of income, although this was not an especially common practice (Housden, 2009).

Manchanda (2006), Human Rights Watch (2007) and Basnet (2005) also confirm recruitment of children in PLA. As per estimates, 3,500 to 4,500 child soldiers were part of the PLA (HRW, 2007). Thousands of children were brought to attend courses in political indoctrination by the Maoists. Later, some of these children became a part of Maoist forces or militia.

The UN Human Rights Monitoring Mission, established to monitor the peace process in Nepal, also found that children were engaged to work for and within the PLA, but at public forums and interviews Maoists denied recruitment of children below 18 years of age (Manchanda, 2006). Having a poor intelligence network, the Royal Nepal Army also used children as informants and to transport food and arms. Many children were tortured and killed by police/RNA on suspicions of their being Maoist supporters (Lawoti & Pahari, 2010).

## Women and the war zone

A significant number of women and young girls had been mobilised by Maoists to develop a base zone, and later women played a crucial role in making many attacks successful.

Uma Bhujel, Sanju, Kamla, Meena Marhatta and Rita V.K. of CPN (Maoist) are known for their courageous tasks and smart planning as they made a tunnel to escape from jail on 30 March 2001 (Bhujel, 2010). Along with some trained women leaders, a large number of unskilled women were also a part of the PLA. Untrained women could

## 96  Schools: the battleground

not defend and escape and were shot dead. The ratio of women killed is high in proportion to women's participation, as women were a part of the lead attack squads.

Women became more vulnerable, as men were either killed or they left the villages to avoid forced recruitment (Manchanda, cited in Lawoti & Pahari, 2010). Women were asked by both RNA and Maoists to transport arms, war materials and food to strategic locations. In a village in Sindhupolchowk, an old woman shared her experience of interacting with PLA members:

> Forty PLA members came and took shelter in my house while 24 others were staying in the house next to mine. They stayed for 14 days. Most of the members of the group had guns but they did not cause any trouble for the villagers. They were carrying medicines and offered these free to needy people in the village.

In Maoist groups, women were responsible for gathering information about the area and institution/place before an attack. Some women Maoist supporters were kidnapped and it was also said that they were raped by policemen. Women were tortured and raped in Maoist camps, especially those women who had a difference of opinion with party leaders or those who wanted to leave the camp. Almost all the women guerrillas who left the Maoists revealed that they were forced to leave due to fear of rape. Similar to experiences in other countries, many cases of gender violence, rape and torture did not come into the public domain even in Nepal (Shakya, 2003).

A few young children and male members who lived in Maoist strongholds joined the insurgents while others left the villages during the peak of the People's War. Women had to manage households, small children and livestock. PLA members and other groups kept moving frequently to attack enemies and avoid encounters, so very often they could come to any house in the night demanding shelter or food. Most of the families residing in remote villages were poor and had only grains/cereals to feed themselves so they refused to offer food to Maoist cadres in many places. Women faced torture when they refused food and support to Maoists (Pradip, 2003).

## Strike, *bandhs* and closure of schools

Children and teachers were forced to attend political rallies in a show of strength for political rivals and create support bases in the community. Since schools were perceived as a functioning of the 'government', political parties asked teachers to shut down schools during political movements.

School children were the key in ensuring the success of a strike or a *bandh* (closure). Children were lead actors in this assignment and also one of the biggest sufferers during the transition.

Frequent calls for *bandhs* by political parties and students unions resulted in a reduced number of school days in an academic year. Some schools, especially those in the Terai, could not function for more than 100 days in an academic year because of political instability. Even after the Comprehensive Peace Agreement of 2006 and elections to the Constituent Assembly in 2008, it was not easy for schools to function normally. In 2009, schools in Saptari district remained open for 154 days instead of the mandatory 220 days (Singer, 2012). It was revealed by a girl student of class 12 in Khungai, Ruphandehi, that whenever Maoists or any political party called for *bandh*, the teachers shut the school. A student in Bajura district recalled incidents of Maoists tearing off books and asking teachers and children to close the school in those days. The closing of schools was common in rural and Maoist-dominated areas.

## 5 Post-People's War
### Complexity and hope

The People's War came to an end on 21 November 2006 as a Comprehensive Peace Accord between the government of Nepal (Seven Party Alliance) and the CPN (Maoist) was signed. Elections to the Constituent Assembly were held in April 2008 and Pushp Kumar Dahal, alias Prachanda, the CPN (Maoist) leader who was also heading PLA during the conflict became the prime minister as CPN-M won the maximum number of seats in the elections.

The Constituent Assembly could not reach a consensus with the different groups and failed to come up with a new constitution for Nepal. So a new assembly election was held in 2013 to carry forward the work of drafting a new constitution. After seven years of efforts, finally Nepal got a new constitution on 20 September 2015. With the formal announcement of the new constitution, some political and identity-based groups (Madheshis and Tharus) started protests in the country; 40 people have been killed in violent incidents, which started with the formal announcement of the new constitution (Haviland, 2015).

Ethnic federalism has been central to the Maoists' agenda, and newly emerged forces representing marginalised populations, in particular the Madhesi parties and Janjati groupings, have also demanded ethnic federalism and formed an unlikely alliance with the Maoists on this. However, the two largest traditional parties – Nepali Congress (NC) and the Communist Party of Nepal (Unified Marxist-Leninist) (UML) – along with smaller right-wing parties, reject ethnic federalism as undermining national unity, meritocracy and individual rights. The Brahmin and Chetri communities of the Hills comprise traditional elite, and an ethnic federal model will certainly reduce their power. This complex political picture reflects a struggle between groups that were disadvantaged and those that were privileged by the old political settlement, with each promoting a federal model that serves its interests (Castillejo, 2013).

Nepal is a democratic republic and has been in transition since 1990. Its citizens still aspire for a stable government which could advance the developmental agenda. Brabant (1998) used transition in terms of economies and found that 'economies in transition' face challenges of stabilisation, privatisation, liberalisation, institution building and developing and maintaining sociopolitical consensus – before examining the evolving role of the state. He also raises issues of integration with the world economy and sustainability of transformation. He found that economies in transition are not always unidirectional or fully moving in the desired direction.

Transition could be the result of either violent or non-violent acts. Even if pushed by non-violent acts, change can be revolutionary as Pareto (1935 quoted in Brabant, 1998) believes, revolution is above all a matter of élite change, whether it happens through violence, civil war or disruption.

Iglic (2003) found pluralisation of political life, formation of new political organisations and new political actions as characteristics of transition. Isajiw (2003) identified the following four characteristics of social transition: (1) transition to a free market economy, (2) transition to a democracy, based on civil society, (3) development of social trust and (4) development of a culture that articulates the basic values and norms, and creates new symbols that reinforce previously suppressed identities and symbols to which all members of a society can comfortably relate to.

Under the Panchayat system, all powers were concentrated in the king and every aspect of life was controlled by the state. No political parties were allowed to function. Citizens' rights and freedom of the press existed on paper but not in reality. If some guests were coming to stay, people had to inform the local police station. The government had its own newspaper and radio, through which it could convey appropriately censored news (Smith, 1981). No one was allowed to criticise the king, or the Panchayat system, as the king supported the status quo. The bureaucracy was lethargic and corrupt. Major control of the economy was in the hands of a very limited number of people who were becoming increasingly rich.

Transition in this chapter indicates a political journey from a party-less Panchayat system to a multi-party democracy and from monarchy to the Democratic Republic of Nepal. These changes bring shifts in the ideology, economy and structure of the state, impacting all walks of life. Sharma (2007) found Nepal in a state of transition marked by increasing awareness among Nepali people about political institutionalisation and a desire to have a pluralistic democracy. He indicated changes in traditional power equations and decreasing relevance of established institutions as indicators of political transition, exemplified by the palace being no more a centre of power. Today, in Nepal political parties, elected representatives are accountable to the people in a changed context. New identities and new organisations are being formed through the process of transition as highlighted by Iglic (2003).

Maoists demanded complete reforms of the education system during the People's War to ensure equity in education (Acharya, 2002), as basic education has been acknowledged widely as a tool of social change (Dreze & Sen, 2003) and issues related to education were the core of the Maoist strategy to fight against monarchy and ensure political changes. Some issues, like education in the mother tongue, were part of the 40-point demand, presented by the Maoists before launching the People's War. Soon after the Comprehensive Peace Agreement (2006) and the formation of the interim government, some changes were made in the education system. In the elections to the Constituent Assembly held in April 2008, CPN (Maoists) emerged as the single largest party and formed the government under the leadership of Prachanda, which was followed by a short-lived government led by CPN (UML). In 2011, CPN (Maoist) again rose to power under the leadership of Baburam Bhattarai. Some of the significant changes, emerging trends and challenges after the transition are discussed in this chapter.

## Changes in the educational scenario

Replacing existing textbooks took time and, thus, making the changes became an impossible task. In 2007, a letter was sent to all the schools with details of the content which should not be taught. A new national anthem was put in place, which is regularly sung in schools. Teaching of Sanskrit has been stopped in government schools. Teachers, who were teaching Sanskrit earlier, teach Nepali now. A new school sector reform plan was developed to be implemented from 2009 to 2015. Some initiatives have been taken up to revise the curriculum, textbooks, restructuring of SMCs and introduction of the mother tongue in the early grades.

## No more *Shri 5 ko Sarkar*; it is *Nepal Sarkar*

The Curriculum Development Centre, Ministry of Education and Sports, Government of Nepal, issued a Government Order (see Annexure I) to all schools and concerned officials after the announcement of House of Representatives-2063 (2007) to revise the content and curriculum of school education with immediate effect. The following recommendations were made by the advisory committee for curriculum, improving the textbooks. These were aimed at teachers and education officials.

> **Box 5.1 Changes suggested in the content of textbooks**
>
> **Subject: social studies (textbook titled *Mero Desh*)**
>
> In place of *Shri 5 ko Sarkar* (Government of His Highness), *Nepal Sarkar* (Government of Nepal) will be used.
>
> The word '*Shahi*' (Royal) will not be used before Nepal Airlines, Nepal Army, Ambassador of Nepal and other related terms during the teaching-learning process.
>
> In place of *Nepal Adhirajya* (Kingdom of Nepal), *Nepal Rajya* (Nepal State) will be used.
>
> *Hindu Adhirajya, Hindu Rajya, Hindu Rastra, Rastriya Dharm Hindu* (Hindu Nation) will be changed to *Dharm Nirpekshya Rajya* (Secular State).
>
> The role of the king, as per the Kingdom's Constitution of 1991, and the provisions of his executive, legislation and judicial powers will be taught in accordance with the provisions made by the House of Representatives in 2007.
>
> Procedures for appointing members of constitutional committees, ambassadors, the Advocate General, Chief of the Army as per the Kingdom's Constitution (1991) will be replaced with provisions made by the House of Representatives (2007) while teaching these concepts.
>
> The national anthem (*Sri Maan Ghambir . . .*) and council of ministers (*Rajya Parishad*) will not be taught.
>
> Only factual and objective content related to the monarchy and the history of the Shah rulers will be taught.
>
> The content will be contextualised in keeping with contemporary changes.
>
> **Changes suggested in the curriculum**
>
> On the first and the last page of textbooks, in place of *Shri 5 ko Sarkar* (Government of His Highness), *Nepal Sarkar* (Government of Nepal) will be used.

In the curriculum, in the preface and the copyright sections, in place of *Shri 5 ko Sarkar* (Government of His Highness), *Nepal Sarkar* (Government of Nepal) will be used.

**Civics and moral education (lower secondary level)**

In the curriculum for class 8, page 3 related to *Rastra and Rastriyata* (Nation and Nationality), *and* on page 12, *Ekata ko Prateek Shri 5* (Symbol of Unity – the King) will not be used.

**Content which must be taught with modifications**

Instead of *Shri 5 ko Sarkar* (Government of the King) mentioned on the first and the last page of the textbooks, *Nepal Sarkar* (Government of Nepal) will be used.

In the Preface and in other places, wherever *Shri 5 ko Sarkar* (Government of the King) has been mentioned, it will be replaced with *Nepal Sarkar* (Government of Nepal).

The picture of the royal family that was added at the beginning of the textbooks will not be used.

Source: Curriculum Development Center, Sanothimi, Bhaktpur: Ministry of Education and Sports, Government of Nepal, sent the letter to all schools and concerned officials after announcement of House of Representatives-2063 (2007) to revise content and curriculum with immediate effects, in public domain.

## New national anthem

The national anthem and Rastriya geet (national songs) played a significant role in translating the vision of the Nepali nation state after the 1960s (Caddell, 2007). The old national anthem of Nepal was opposed by the Maoists as it praised the king as Almighty. So, it was replaced in August 2007 by a new national anthem, which is now incorporated in school textbooks.

## Towards fulfilling the promises made under the 40-point charter of demands

The 40-point charter of demands was presented before the government in February 1996, in which the Maoists asked for education in the mother tongue, a unified education system, free education up to secondary level, special support to orphans and disabled and gender equity among others.

Some of the changes that have come about include:

- Free textbooks are now being given up to the 10th standard.
- An interim constitution and School Sector Reforms Plan (2009) with emphasis on the right to free education up to secondary level (Government of Nepal, 2009) has been set up.
- Textbooks are being revised and now represent a changed political ideology and gender perspectives.
- A new textbook for social science for 9th standard has a special chapter on equal participation of women in development.

## Politics of photographs

The photograph of the royal family was torn off during the People's War and now the new social science textbook for class 10th has a chapter on the Comprehensive Peace Agreement of 2006. In this chapter, a photograph of Maoist leader Prachanda and the then Prime Minister G.P. Koirala is given showing them signing the peace treaty. This might just be an indication of the circulation of elites and the hegemony of a new regime.

## New provisions for SMCs

SMCs are being constituted for a three-year term. An executive committee composed of 10 members takes the decisions. This committee includes representatives of women and different communities. The headmaster works as the secretary. SMCs are more empowered and are functioning in a decentralised manner. Earlier, committee members were appointed by district officials on the basis of connections with Panchayat representatives or personnel of the royal government. But now, a majority of the members are elected by parents and the local community.

## Education provision in the interim constitution, 2007

The provision for education in the Interim Constitution, 2007 (Section 3, Article 18 of Democratic Republic of Nepal) includes:

- Right to education and culture of each citizen has been provisioned as a fundamental right.
- Each community has a right to protect its own language, script and culture.

- Each community can operate primary schools with the mother tongue as the medium of instruction.
- Provisions will be made to ensure free education up to the secondary level.

## A new integrated school system

An integrated school system has been proposed and is being implemented gradually as schools are being upgraded from primary to elementary and so on. The senior secondary level is being integrated with the school system (it was a part of higher education earlier). Structural integration of classes 1st to 5th with 6th to 8th in schools is believed to improve students' performance with the introduction of a competency-based learning programme. The integrated structure will minimise dropouts, as it provides inter-linkages which were not there earlier. SMCs can also play an effective role in an integrated school system in planning and monitoring.

Integration of art and craft skills from 6th standard onwards has also been proposed under the School Sector Reform Plan, 2009.

## Recruitment of teachers

The Department of Education has estimated a shortage of about 60,000 teachers in the school system (SSRP, 2009). Now teacher recruitment will be done through a centralised process and only candidates with a teacher's license will be recruited. SMCs have been given a significant role in teacher management. Provisions have been made to give a budget to the SMCs, so that they can send school teachers for need-based in-service training.

The minimum qualifications for teachers for basic education will be higher secondary in place of secondary school. In teacher recruitment, women, Dalits and other disadvantaged groups will be given priority to address issues of gender and social exclusion (SSRP, 2009).

> The National Centre for Educational Development (NCED) is conducting certification and recurrent training courses for primary and secondary level teachers through Education Training Centres (ETCs) located at different places in the country and through other allied training-providers. Completion of a professional teacher training course has been made mandatory, prior to entering the teaching profession.
>
> (SSRP, 2009, p. 37)

## Addressing the language issue

In Nepal leading political parties have been promising to do justice with the regional languages and representation of the other languages along with Nepali in textbooks. After the monarchy came to an end, some efforts have been made to develop textbooks in local languages. Awadhi has been incorporated as an optional subject in the early grades. A textbook in Awadhi for standard 1 (*Hamar Bhasha*) was introduced during the academic session of 2009–10. The initiative was appreciated in international forums, especially by multilingual education groups. However, during my field visits to schools in an Awadhi speaking area, I found that the Awadhi textbook is not being used by the teachers. In the 2010–11 academic session, the Awadhi textbook did not reach the schools, so English was taught as an optional subject in 1st standard. Many parents prefer English to Awadhi. They believe English will provide better opportunities to their children.

## Framework for schools as zones of peace

Recognising education as a fundamental right of the child and a responsibility of the government, in May 2011, the Ministry of Education presented a framework for schools as 'Zones of Peace' (UNICEF, 2012), which was approved by the cabinet (see Appendix). A code of conduct is being developed to ensure smooth functioning of schools in an inclusive and non-threatening manner.

## Provisions of scholarships for children of martyrs

The School Sector Reform Plan of 2009 has proposed scholarships for the children of martyrs' families (who sacrificed their lives during the People's War) along with scholarships for girl students, Dalits, the disabled and girls from the Karnali region. Dalit students will get Nepali Rupia 350 per year and children of martyrs will be given Nepali Rupia 1,000 per year.

## Ray of hope

The new era demands a new social contract, as the forces that fought against the monarchy now lead the state and have a new constitutional framework. Political parties mistrust each other and are struggling with factions within the parties, which lead not only to political instability but uncertainty on finalising the constitution of the country. If the political parties fail at solidarity on issues of national importance, the country will have to manage with limited resources and high aspirations, and it may fail to address issues of development, welfare and essential services, and would go into chaos.

Past experiences have proved that 'where transitions remained disputed, the State lost its capacity to enforce the rule of law, even if it managed to hang on to power' (Mungiu-Pippidi, 2010).

Evidence gathered from primary and secondary sources reveals that certain groups were deprived of resources and were denied opportunities in an organised manner at various levels. This was not limited to stray instances but has a long history of biased practices. The nature of the exploitative cycle was interlinked and distinct at the same time. The country was a proclaimed Hindu nation having 80 per cent believers in Hinduism. This religious identity of the nation not only helped the monarch and elites to protect their privileged positions but also to maintain opportunity gaps. The privileged groups legitimised many of the exclusionary practices through religion. Any act or criticism of the king was not only unacceptable in the country during their rule, but was also banned by constitutional provisions. As mentioned in previous chapters the caste-based social structure was sanctioned by the religious identity of the nation and helped Bahuns, Chetris, Thakuris, Newars and other upper caste communities to exploit educational services and opportunities in their favour.

Tumin (1985, p. 39) rightly articulated that

> when religion is the dominant institution – as in medieval church and modern fundamentalist states such as Iran – the highest rewards, power, prestige as well as property, are likely to be awarded to the chief religious specialists such as bishops, cardinals, caliphs and imams.

In the case of Nepal, the kings were Chetri by caste and enjoyed the supreme religious position as the living form of Lord Vishnu. They enjoyed the highest rewards, power, prestige and property. The Bahuns, being the priest class, also benefited with rewards, power, prestige and property.

Though upper-caste supremacy was very evident, it was also combined with a regional identity, so the most beneficial groups of these castes were from the Hill region rather than from the Terai. The Bahuns and Chetris of Terai only received benefits and opportunities in their region, which were relatively less attractive or were given up by Bahuns and Chetris of the Hill region in the absence of options available within their own clan. People of the Terai, who constitute more than 35 per cent of the population, had a feeling of being second-class citizens as they have been raising issues of low representation in army, civil services and in the political process as well for quite some time now. In contrast, Newars who accounted for only 5.6 per cent of the total population and were highly concentrated in and around Kathmandu had occupied as much as 36 per cent of the civil service positions in the 1990s (Rana, 1998).

School norms were made on the basis of regions and raised many questions. Before 2007, the pupil-teacher ratio (PTR) stipulated for the mountain and for the Terai region was not equal. Now Nepal is going to be divided into seven regions to ensure inclusive development.

Along with regional discrimination, social mobility was limited even after the abolition of the Panchayat system. Further, there was also poor representation of Dalits and other backward castes in the education system. This low representation of socially excluded groups came from lack of access and participation at the school level. The challenges before the children were not only in accessing schools in the neighbourhood but also poverty and discrimination in the schools. It was confirmed by many respondents that upper-caste people (including teachers) preferred to send their children to private schools, and now consider government schools for children of *nanh jaati* (lower caste). A fifth of the children in Nepal now attend private schools and the proportion of children enrolling in private schools is increasing.

Language was another dimension of exclusion, as previously Sanskrit and later Nepali, were the medium of instruction. Since learning Sanskrit was of professional significance for Bahuns, as they had to perform religious rituals, they capitalised on the opportunities in literacy and education as well. Both Sanskrit and Nepali were not in practice among a sizeable number of Nepali people, so they accepted their poor educational attainments as a personal failure, rather than being victims of a discriminatory system. Bourdieu (1986) reminds of the 'cultural capital' which students must acquire uniformly. So, the working class children find success harder, as they have to learn a new culture, practices and language.

The political scenario was a reflection of the stratified society of Nepal. In most of the cases, political competition was between the leaders of upper castes. A majority of the senior leaders of political parties were either Bahun or Chetri and, therefore, it was a real challenge for the Dalits/Janjatis to claim their rightful political space (Gellner, 2007). Though the state claims to serve all citizens, in reality only the interests of the powerful groups are protected while the marginalised groups get symbolic space instead of actual power positions (Sears, 2008).

While the People's War was at its peak from 2002 to 2005, the Seventh Amendment of Education Act (Ministry of Education and Sports, 2004) was enforced with provisions for adopting community schools as a system of education, free education in community primary schools, teacher training and teacher licensing, de-politicisation of the teaching force, regulation of private schools, and free education and incentives for Dalit children. Through the new amendment, the government attempted to encounter the Maoists' allegations of injustice and the denial of rights and tried to attract the marginalised sections in their favour. This way, both the parties at war against each other kept education at the centre of their strategies in an attempt to influence communities and mobilise them to their side. Maoists also introduced their own calendar in 20 to 25 schools, and asked teachers to declare holidays on Labour Day and on Mao's birthday (Basnet, 2005).

The huge expectation of the people based on the promises made by political leaders has emerged as a new challenge in the country. One group of the Maoists cadres has already left the CPN (Maoists) and formed another group under the leadership of Mohan Vaidya. This group keeps opposing and exposing its old comrades and has also threatened to enter into a war against the new political regime.

Teachers are divided on party lines and some more associations have been formed after the People's War. Family members of those who were killed during the People's War have not forgotten their wounds.

The Ministry of Education has been working on school sector reforms. Favouring multilingual education, it is working on producing a new set of textbooks. It also has provisions for incentives for marginalised children and for teacher training. But, as there has hardly been any restructuring of the old administrative system, it is unlikely that there will be many positive changes for learners studying in government schools.

Enrolments, retention and quality of learning are major challenges, in addition to generating faith among the parents in the education system, with more than 50 per cent untrained, poorly paid and politicised teachers. Restructuring of the bureaucracy is an imperative, keeping the issues of social exclusion and the need for ensuring equal opportunities for all in perspective. For such a restructuring to take place, a stable government is required with enough resources. However, the leadership of all the leading parties is still in the hands of Bahuns and Chetris/Thakuris. Some changes have been proposed in education, but on the whole, it seems that power has been transferred from one group of elites to another within the clan, as both the prime ministers of CPN (Maoist), Prachanda and Baburam Bhattarai, are 'Bahuns' like G.P. Koirala, who served as prime minister in Nepal for the longest period of time. This is a case of 'circulation of elites' as stated by Pareto, which is a clue for maintaining equilibrium in society as well (Delaney, 1971).

Provisions have been made for the reservation and promotion of Dalits, Janjati groups and women in administration and education services. But relative instability and high expectations from the government are the major challenges on the political front. In a society with a complex social structure, it will always be a test for the government to justify actions and decide who is entitled to enjoy the biggest share of property and power (Tumin, 1985).

In education, ensuring equal opportunities for all the social groups and establishing forward institutional linkages should be the priority for the government because education plays a crucial role in developing human capital, which results in economic growth and individual benefits (Judson, 1998). The National Framework for Capacity Development has been prepared and recognised as an essential means of ensuring quality education through the School Sector Reform Plan for 2009 (SSRP, 2009).

Tawil (2002), however, warns that educational policymaking in the context of uncertain peace and instability is a challenge, and high unemployment could be a threat to sustainable peace, particularly in post-conflict situations. The anger of the youth groups, students and ordinary people in general is rising, with political uncertainty and frequent calls for *bandhs*. Fresh incidents of violence after 20 September 2015 are also of concern, as some groups have been demanding amendments to the newly introduced constitution.

The economic and educational status of the country cannot be improved without political stability. The issue of unemployment, if not tackled quickly, could be a threat to sustainable peace, particularly in the post-conflict phase (Tawil, 2002). Educational policymaking in the context of uncertain peace and relative instability is a big task for the government in power.

On the issues of ethnic representation and language, Nepal must project and protect a common identity internally and externally. If Nepal fails to do so, formation of a new social contract will be difficult to achieve, and it will collapse like all the other three post-communist federations – USSR, Yugoslavia and Czechoslovakia – collapsed (Mungiu-Pippidi, 2010).

# Annexure I
## Letter to revise curriculum and content

*Government of Nepal, Ministry of Education and Sports, Curriculum Development Center, Sanothimi, Bhaktput*

Letter sent to all schools and concerned officials after announcement of House of Representatives-2063 (2007) to revise content and curriculum with immediate effects. The following recommendations were given by curriculum, textbooks improvement advisory committee to teachers and education officials.

- In place of '*Shri 5 ko Sarkar*' (Government of his highness), *Nepal Sarkar* (Government of Nepal) will be used.
- The word '*Shahi*' (Royal) would not be used before Nepal Airlines, Nepal Army, Ambassador of Nepal and other related terms during teaching learning process.
- In place of '*Nepal Adhirajya*' (Kingdom of Nepal), *Nepal Rajya* (Nepal state) would be used.
- In spite of *Hindu Adhirajya, Hindu Rajya, Hindu Rastra, Rastriya Dharm Hindu* (Hindu Nation) will be changed to *Dharm Nirpekshya Rajya* (Secular State).
- Role of the king as per Kingdom's constitution 2047 (1991) and provisions of executive, legislation and judiciary would be changed with provisions made by House of Representatives-2063 (2007) while teaching text.
- Procedures of appointing members of constitutional committees, ambassadors, Advocate General, Chief of Army as per Kingdom's constitution 2047 (1991) would be replaced with provisions made by House of Representatives-2063 (2007) while teaching these concepts.

- Existing National Anthem (*Rastragaan*) and council of ministers (*Rajya Parishad*) would not be taught.
- Only factual and objective content related with monarchy and history of Shah rulers will be taught.
- Considering the contemporary change, content would be contextualised to teach.

## Suggested changes in curriculum

- On the first and last page of the curriculum, in place of '*Shri 5 ko Sarkar*' (Government of his highness), *Nepal Sarkar* (Government of Nepal) will be used.
- In curriculum, in preface and in copyright sections, in place of '*Shri 5 ko Sarkar*' (Government of his highness), *Nepal Sarkar* (Government of Nepal) will be used.

## Change in social science textbook

- In 8th chapter of class 6th, *Rajmukut ra Rashtriyagaan* (Crown and National Anthem) would not be taught.

## Civics and moral education (lower secondary level)

- In the curriculum of class 8th, page 3, related with *Rastra and Rastriyata* (Nation and Nationality), and on page 12, *ekata ko prateek sri 5* (symbol of unity the king) would not be used.

## Content which must be taught with modification

- Instead of '*Shri 5 ko Sarkar*' (Government of the King) mentioned on first and last page of the textbooks, *Nepal Sarkar* (Government of Nepal) will be used.
- Preface and other places wherever '*Shri 5 ko Sarkar*' (Government of the King) has been mentioned would be replaced with *Nepal Sarkar* (Government of Nepal).
- Don't use picture of royal family, added in the beginning of textbook.

Suggested changes in the content of textbooks

| Class | Page number | Words/content which will be replaced | New suggested/ alternate words/ concept |
|---|---|---|---|
| Subject: Mero Desh/social studies | | | |
| 4th *Mero Desh* | 28 | Shri 5 ko Sarkar | Nepal Sarkar |
| 4th *Mero Desh* | 46 | Shahi | Don't use |
| 4th *Mero Desh* | 130 | Rastriya Sabha ko Gathan Prakriya (Formation of National Assembly) | Don't teach |
| 4th *Mero Desh* | 131 | Karya Palika Gathan Prakriya (Formation of Executive Body) | Don't teach |
| 4th *Mero Desh* | 135 | Pradhan Nayadheesh ko Niyukti Prakriya Chapter 7, selection of chief justice | Don't teach |
| 5th *Mero Desh* | 95 and 96 | Karya Palika Gathan Prakriya (Formation of Executive Body) | Don't teach |
| 5th *Mero Desh* | 98 and 102 | Shri 5 ko Sarkar | Nepal Sarkar |
| 6th | 4 and 6 | Shri 5 ko Sarkar | Nepal Sarkar |
| 6th | 4 | Nepal Adhirajya | Nepal Sarkar |
| 6th | 32 | Rastriya Dharm Hindu | Nepal Dharm Nirpekshya Rastra |
| 6th | 36 | Rajmukut and Rastragaan | Don't teach |
| 6th | 37 | Activity No. 2 *Rajmukut Bhayeka* – and activity No. 7 *Rastriya gaan gayer sunau* | Don't teach |
| 7th | 30, 31 and 42 | Terminology – *Hindu Rajya, Hindu Rastra, Rastriya Dharm Hindu* | *Dharm Nirpekshya* (Secular nation) |
| 7th | 56 | Shri 5 ko Sarkar | Nepal Sarkar |
| 7th | 56 | In first and second section – Nepal ko Nagrik hune cha | Don't teach |
| 7th | 59 | Meaning of word – *Adhirajya* | Don't teach |
| 8th | 3 and 17 | Shri 5 ko Sarkar | Nepal Sarkar |

| Class | Page number | Words/content which will be replaced | New suggested/ alternate words/ concept |
|---|---|---|---|
| 8th | 18 and 37 | Term 'Sahi' before Airlines etc. | Remove it |
| 8th | 58, 59 and 94 | Adhirajya | Nepal Rajya |
| 8th | 62 to 68 | Content related with Karya Palika, Nayapalika, Vyvasthapika | Don't teach |
| 9th | 4, 6, 18, 21 and 26 | Shri 5 ko Sarkar | Nepal Sarkar |
| 9th | 26 | Nepal Adhirajya | Nepal Rajya |
| 9th | Section 2 | | Don't teach |
| 9th | 35 | Activity no. 2 | Don't teach |
| 9th | 64 and 65 | Nepal ko vartman samvidhan ko viseshta haru | Don't teach |
| 9th | 202 | Sahi Nepali Sena | Nepali Sena |
| 10th | Various pages | Shri 5 ko Sarkar | Nepal Sarkar |
| 10th | 62 to 67 | Nepal ma samvaidhanik rajtantra, vyavasthapika, karyapalika related chapters | Don't teach |
| 10th | 70, 71 | Samvaidhanik angaharu | Don't teach |
| 10th | 72 | Sri 5 baata – -niyukti garibakshnch | Don't teach |
| 10th | 75 | Nepal Adhirajya | Nepal Rajya |
| 10th | 82 | Pahila ra pancho bunda | Don't teach |
| **Subject: Nepali** | | | |
| 9th | 71 | Srijanatmak abhhyaas rahe ko rajmukut sirsakma prabandh lekhne kriyakalap | Replace with content on nationality |
| **Subject: English** | | | |
| 5th | 164 | His Majesty's Government of Nepal | Government of Nepal |
| 9th and 10th | Pages inside | HMGN | |

# Annexure II
## Countries affected with conflict

### 1999–2008 and 2002–2011
Afghanistan
Algeria
Angola*
Burundi
Central African Republic
Chad
Colombia
Cote d'Ivoire
Democratic Republic of Congo
Eretria*
Ethiopia
Georgia*
Guinea*
India
Indonesia
Iran**
Iraq
Liberia
Libya**
Mali**
Myanmar
Nepal
Niger**
Nigeria
Pakistan
Occupied Palestinian territory
Philippines
Russian Federation

Rwanda*
Serbia*
Sierra Leone*
Somalia
Sri Lanka
Sudan
Syria**
Thailand
Timor-Leste*
Turkey
Uganda
Yemen

Note: Countries with single asterisk mark * were on the list in 2011 but no longer identified as conflict affected in 2013. Countries with double asterisk marks ** joined the list in 2013.

Source: Save the Children, 2013 – Attacks on Education

# References

Acharya, U. D. (2002). *Primary education in Nepal, policy, problems and prospects* (p. 100). Kathmandu: Ekta Books.

Adriaensens, D. (2010, May 11). Dismantling the Iraqi state. *NSPM*. Retrieved from www.nspm.rs/nspm-in-english/dismantling-the-iraqi-state.html

Aguilar, P., Retamal, G., & International Bureau of Education. (1998). *Rapid educational response in complex emergencies: A discussion document*. UNESCO. Retrieved from www.ibe.unesco.org/fileadmin/user_upload/archive/publications/free_publications/Retamal.pdf

Anandy, Nepal Sadbhavana Party. (2008, January 26). *Public meeting*. Nepal, Padariya.

Andersen, G. (2007, June 28). Future schools: Let's put money and energy into education. *Nepali Times*. Retrieved from www.nepalitimes.com/issue/354/GuestColumn/13650

Apple, M. W. (Ed.). (1982). *Cultural and economic reproduction in education: Essays on class, ideology and the state* (p. 362). New York: Routledge & Kegan Paul.

Ashby, J. A. (1985). Equity and discrimination among children: Schooling decisions in rural Nepal. *Comparative Education Review*, 29(1), 68–79. Retrieved from www.jstor.org/stable/1188143

Atkinson, P. (1995). Some perils of paradigms. *Qualitative Health Research*, 5, 117–124.

Badescu, G., & Uslaner, E. M. (Eds.). (2003). *Social capital and transition to democracy* (p. 239). London: Routledge.

Barash, D. P., & Webel, C. P. (2002). *Peace and conflict studies*. Thousand Oaks: SAGE.

Barash, D. P., & Webel, C. P. (2009). *The reasons for wars: Ideological, social and economic levels, peace and conflict studies*. Thousand Oaks, CA: SAGE Publications.

Basnet, D. (Producer). (2005). *Schools in the cross fire* [DVD].

BBC News. (2011, May 17). *Rwanda: How the genocide happened*. Retrieved from www.bbc.com/news/world-africa-13431486

BBC. (2012). Nepal profile [Web series episode]. *BBC Nepal*. London: BBC. Retrieved from www.bbc.co.uk/news/world-south-asia-12499391

# References

Berry, C. (2010). Working effectively with non-state actors to deliver education in fragile states. *Development in Practice, 20*(4–5: Achieving Education for All through public private partnership?).

Bhattarai, B. (2003). *The nature of underdevelopment and regional structure of Nepal, a marxist analysis* (p. 537). New Delhi: Adroit Publishers.

Bhujel, U. (2010). *Bandh diwaron se khule akash tak* (Translated from Nepali by V. Sharma) (p. 136). Noida: Samkaleen Tisari Duniya.

Bikash, L. (2005). *Foreign donors suspend aid to Nepal, fewer grants from abroad could spell economic trouble.* Retrieved from http://english.ohmynews.com/articleview/article_view.asp?menu=c10400&no=239466&rel_no=1

Bird, L. (2003). *Surviving school: Education for refugee children from Rwanda* (p. 140). Paris: IIEP, UNESCO.

Bista, D. B. (1991). *Fatalism and development: Nepal's struggle for modernization.* Nepal: Orient Blackswan.

Blin, A. (2011, June). Armed groups and intra-state conflicts: The dawn of a new era? *International Review of the Red Cross, 93*(882), 287–310. Retrieved from www.icrc.org/eng/assets/files/review/2011/irrc-882-blin.pdf

Bourdieu, P. (1986). *The forms of capital.* Retrieved from http://en.wikipedia.org/wiki/Sociology_of_education

Brabant, J. M. V. (1998). *The political economy of transition: Coming to grips with history and methodology* (p. 559). London: Routledge.

Buchmann, C., & Hannum, E. (2001). Education and stratification in developing countries: A review of theories and research. *Annual Review of Sociology, 27,* 77–102. Retrieved from www.jstor.org/stable/2678615

The Bureau of Publications College of Education. (1956). *Education in Nepal: Report of the Nepal National Education Planning Commission* (1st ed.). Kathmandu: The Bureau of Publications College of Education.

Burghart, R. (1993). The political culture of Panchayat democracy. In M. Hutt (Ed.), *Nepal in the nineties* (pp. 1–13). New Delhi: Oxford University Press.

Bush, K. D., & Saltarelli, D. (2000). *The two faces of education in ethnic conflict towards a peace building education for children* (p. 45). Florence: UNICEF (International Child Development Centre).

Caddell, M. (2007). A historical perspective on schooling, development, and Nepali nation-state. In K. Krishna & J. Oesterheld (Eds.), *Education and social change in South Asia* (pp. 251–284). New Delhi: Orient Longman.

Carney, S., Bista, M., & Agergaard, J. (2007). Empowering the 'local' through education? Exploring community-managed schooling in Nepal. *Oxford Review of Education, 33*(5), 611–628. Retrieved from www.jstor.org/stable/20462361

Castillejo, C. (2013). Gender and statebuilding. In T. D. Sisk & D. Chandler (Eds.), *Routledge handbook of international statebuilding.* Oxford: Routledge.

"Children in Maoist Ranks," *Kathmandu Post.* (June 17, 2004). In: Watchlist. (2005). *Caught in the middle: Mounting violations against children in Nepal's armed conflict.* Retrieved from http://watchlist.org/caught-in-the-middle-mounting-violations-against-children-in-Nepals-armed-conflict/

# References

CNN. (2015). *Syrian civil war fast facts*. Retrieved from http://edition.cnn.com/2013/08/27/world/meast/syria-civil-war-fast-facts/index.html [Accessed 10 October 2015] and www.ohchr.org/EN/ProfessionalInterest/Pages/CRC.aspx

Communist Party of Nepal (Maoist). (2007). *Pratibadhata-patra: Naya Nepal nimit naya vichar r naya netritva*. Kathmandu: Communist Party of Nepal (Maoist).

Communist Party of Nepal (UML). (1994). *Election manifesto for mid-term poll '94*. Kathmandu: Central Committee.

Conteh-Morgan, E. (2004). *Collective political violence* (p. 323). London: Routledge.

Cowan, S. (2015, April 21). The maharaja and the monarch: Two visits to United Kingdom in different era. *The Record*. Retrieved from http://www.recordnepal.com/wire/maharaja-and-monarch-0/

Conteh-Morgan, E. (2005). *Collective political violence: An introduction to the theories and cases of violent conflicts*. New York: Routledge.

Creswell, J. W. (2003). *Research design: Qualitative, quantitative and mixed methods approaches* (2nd ed.). London: Sage Publications Inc.

CWIN. (2005). *Effect of armed conflict on children in Nepal*. Retrieved from www.cwin-nepal.org

CWIN. (2007). *The girl child in Nepal*. Retrieved from www.cwin.org.np/index.php?option=com_content&view=article&id=65:the-girl-child-in-Nepal&lang=en

CWIN. (2009). *Conflict affected children (1996–2006)*. Retrieved from www.cwin.org.np/index.php?option=com_jdownloads&Itemid=15&lang=en

Davies, L. (2004). *Education and conflict: Complexity and chaos* (p. 242). London: Routledge.

Delamont, S. (2008). Analytical perspective in collecting and interpreting qualitative materials. In N. K. Denzin & Y. S. Lincoln (Eds.), *Collecting and interpreting qualitative materials* (p. 682). Thousand Oaks, CA: SAGE.

Delaney, S. J. (1971, July). Pareto's theory of elites and education. Studium: The Bulletin of the School of Education, 3(1). Retrieved from http://hkjo.lib.hku.hk/archive/files/040d96e164080dd1e2baca9d7d53187d.pdf

Deutsch, M. (1973). *Resolution of conflict: Constructive and destructive processes*. New Haven, CT: Yale University Press.

Dhungel, D. N. (1998). The history of Nepal. In D. N. Dhungel & P. S. Rana (Eds.), *In contemporary Nepal* (pp. 14–42). Delhi: Vikas Publishing House.

Dreze, J., & Sen, A. (2003). Basic education as a political issue. In J. Tilak (Ed.), *Education, society, and development: National and international perspectives* (pp. 3–48). New Delhi: APH Publishing Corporation.

Eck, K. (2010). Recruiting rebels: Indoctrination and political education in Nepal. In M. Lawoti & A. Karki (Eds.), *Maoist Insurgency in Nepal* (pp. 33–52). London: Routledge.

Education vs education. (2005, July 29). *Nepali Times*, 11.

The eight point SPA-Maoist agreement. (2007, April 24). *Telegraphnepal.com*. Retrieved from www.telegraphnepal.com/backup/telegraph/news

# References

Emmons, K. (2001). *EAPRO: Adult wars, child soldiers: Voices of children involved in armed conflict in the East Asia and Pacific Region.* Retrieved from www.unicef.org/evaldatabase/index_15350.html [Accessed 10 October 2015].

Fisher, R. J., & Kishley, L. (1991). The potential complementarity of mediation and consultation within a contingency model of third party consultation. *Journal of Peace Research, 28*(1), 29–42.

Fontana, A., & Frey, J. H. (2005). The interview: From neutral stance to political involvement. In N. K. Denzin & Y. S. Lincoln (Eds.), *The Sage handbook of qualitative research* (pp. 695–728). Thousand Oaks, CA: SAGE.

"Four Maoist killed," *Kathmandu post daily.* (September 9, 2004). In: Watchlist. (2005). On their report "Mounting violations against children in Nepal's armed conflict". Retrieved from http://watchlist.org/caught-in-the-middle-mounting-violations-against-children-in-Nepals-armed-conflict/

Gaige, F., & Scholz, J. (1991). Parliamentary elections in Nepal: Political freedom and stability. *Asian Survey, 31*(11), 1040–1060. Retrieved from www.jstor.org/stable/2645306

Galtung, J. (1990). Cultural violence. *Journal of Peace Research, 27*(3), 291–305. Retrieved from http://journals.sagepub.com/doi/abs/10.1177/0022343390027003005

Galtung, J. (1998). *Violence, war, and their impact.* Retrieved from https://them.polylog.org/5/fgj-en.htm

Gautam, S. (2004, March 28). *Armed conflict in Nepal and Nepali press.* Retrieved from www.fesnepal.org/reports/2004/seminar_reports/papers_ESN/paper_shobha.htm

Gellner, D. N. (Ed.). (2007). *Resistance and the state: Nepalese experience* (p. 383). Oxford: Berghahn Books.

Gibbs, A. (1997). *Social research update: Focus groups.* London: Guilford.

Glasl, F. (1982). The process of conflict escalations and role of third parties. In G. B. Peterson (Ed.), *Conflict management and industrial relations* (pp. 119–140). Boston: Kluwer-Nijhoff.

Global Coalition to Protect Education From Attack (GCPEA). (2014). *Education under attack 2014.* Retrieved from http://www.protectingeducation.org/education-under-attack-2014

Global Movement for Children Afghanistan Working Group. (2001). *Lost chances: The changing situation of children in Afghanistan, 1990–2000.* Retrieved from http://reliefweb.int/sites/reliefweb.int/files/resources/EBBBE884F6CE5172C1256ACB003505E8-gmc-afg-30jun.pdf

Government of Nepal. (1956). *The five year plan for education in Nepal.* Kathmandu: Bureau of Publications.

Government of Nepal. (2003). *Education for all 2004–2009: Core document.* Kathmandu: Ministry of Education and Sports.

Government of Nepal. (2007a). *Research and educational information management section: A glimpse.* Kathmandu: Ministry of Education and Sports.

# References

Government of Nepal. (2007b). *School sector reform plan*. Kathmandu: Ministry of Education & Sports.

Government of Nepal. (2007c). *Technical review of school education in Nepal-2006: Third round survey report*. Kathmandu: TRSE.

Government of Nepal. (2008a). *Hamar Bhasha – Class 1*. Bhaktapur: Pathyakram Vikas Kendra, Ministry of Education.

Government of Nepal. (2008b). *The interim constitution of Nepal, 2007*. Retrieved from www.nic.gov.np/download/interim-constitution.pdf

Government of Nepal. (2009). *School sector reform plan 2009–2015*. Kathmandu: Ministry of Education.

Government of Nepal. (2010). *National framework for capacity development*. Kathmandu: Ministry of Education.

Government of Nepal. (2011a). *District profile of Rupandehi*. Retrieved from www.ddcrupandehi.gov.np

Government of Nepal. (2011b). *Flash report–2011: Key findings*. Kathmandu: Ministry of Education.

Government of Nepal. (2012a). *National framework for schools as zones of peace*. Presentation in International Seminar on Schools as Zones of Peace, 9–11 May 2012, Hotel Summit, Sanepa, Kathmandu, Nepal.

Government of Nepal. (2012b). *National population census 2011*. Retrieved from www.cbs.gov.np/2012

Government of Nepal, Curriculum Development Center. (2005). *National curriculum for school education framework*. Bhaktapur: Ministry of Education and Sports.

Gross, O., & Ni Aolain, F. (2006). *Law in times of crisis: Emergency powers in theory and practice*. Cambridge: Cambridge University Press.

Government of Nepal, Ministry of Education and Sports. (2006). *Mero Desh-class 5*. Bhaktapur: Pathyakram Vikas Kendra.

Gurr, T. C. (1968). A causal model of civil strife: A comparative analysis using new indices. *American Political Science Review*, 62, 1104–1124.

Hachhethu, K. (2007a). Legitimacy crisis of Nepali monarchy. *Economic & Political Weekly*, 42(20), 1828–1833.

Hachhethu, K. (2007b). Social change and leadership: A study of Bhaktapur city. In D. N. Gellner, K. Nawa, & H. Ishii (Eds.), *Political and social transformations in north India and Nepal* (pp. 63–90). Delhi: Manohar Publications.

Hangen, S. I. (2010). *The rise of ethnic politics in Nepal: Democracy in the margins* (p. 190). London: Routledge.

Haq, E. (1992). Open education in a closed society: A study in social and educational inequalities in contemporary India. In D. Gupta (Ed.), *Social stratification* (p. 461). New Delhi: Oxford University Press.

Haviland, C. (2015, September 19). Why is Nepal's new constitution controversial? *BBC News*. Retrieved from http://www.bbc.com/news/world-asia-34280015

Höfer, A. (1979). *The caste hierarchy and the state of Nepal: A study of the Muluki Ain of 1854*. Innsbruck: Wagner.

Hoftun, M. (1993). The dynamics and chronology of the 1990 revolution. In M. Hutt (Ed.), *Nepal in nineties* (pp. 15–27). New Delhi: Oxford University Press.

## References

Holstein, J. A., & Gubrium, J. F. (1995). *The active interview* (p. 85). Thousand Oaks, CA: SAGE.

Holton, R. J., & Turner, B. S. (1986). *Talcott Parsons on economy and society* (p. 276). New York: Routledge & Kegan Paul.

Housden, O. (2009). In a weak state status and reintegration of Children Associated with Armed forces and Armed Groups (CAAFAG) in Nepal. *Institute of Peace and Conflict Studies (IPCS), India*. Retrieved from http://www.ipcs.org/pdf_file/issue/RP20-Oli-Final.pdf

Human Rights Watch. (2007). *Children in the ranks: The Maoists' use of child soldiers in Nepal*. Human Rights Watch. Retrieved from www.hrw.org/news/2007

Human Rights Watch. (2009). *Sabotaged schooling: Naxalite attacks and police occupation of schools in India's Bihar and Jharkhand states*. Human Rights Watch. Retrieved from www.hrw.org/en/reports/2009/12/09/sabotaged-schooling-0

Human Rights Watch. (2012). *World Report 2012*. Retrieved from https://www.hrw.org/world-report/2012

Human Security Research Group. (2012). *Human security report 2012*. Vancouver, Canada: Human Security Press. Retrieved from https://reliefweb.int/sites/reliefweb.int/files/resources/2012HumanSecurityReport-FullText_0.pdf

Hutmacher, W. (2002). Education systems, social integration and inequality. In S. Tawil (Ed.), *Curriculum change and social inclusion* (pp. 14–25). Geneva: UNESCO-IBE.

Hutt, M. (1994). Drafting the 1990 constitution. In M. Hutt (Ed.), *Nepal in the nineties: Versions of the past, visions of the future*. New Delhi: Oxford University Press.

Hutt, M. (2001). Drafting the 1990 constitution. In M. Hutt (Ed.), *Nepal in the nineties* (pp. 28–47). New Delhi: Oxford University Press.

Hutt, M. (2004). Monarchy, democracy and Maoism in Nepal. In M. Hutt (Ed.), *Himalayan People's War: Nepal's Maoist rebellion* (pp. 1–20). Bloomington: Indiana University Press.

Iglic, H. (2003). Trust networks and democratic transition Yugoslavia in the mid-1980s. In G. Badescu & E. M. Uslaner (Eds.), *Social capital and the transition to democracy* (pp. 10–27). London: Routledge.

INSECOnline. Retrieved from http://www.inseconline.org

International Alert. (2006). *Nepal at a crossroads*. Retrieved from www.international-alert.org/sites/default/.../Nepal_at_crossroads.pdf

International Committee of the Red Cross. (2010). *Protocols additional to the Geneva conventions of August 12, 1949*. Retrieved from https://www.icrc.org/eng/assets/files/other/icrc_002_0321.pdf

IRIN News. (2006). *Between two stones*. Decades of Damage to Education Series. Retrieved from www.irinnews.org/film/4114/Between-Two-Stones

Isajiw, W. W. (Ed.). (2003). *Society in transition: Social change in Ukraine in western perspectives* (p. 433). Toronto: Canadian Scholars' Press Inc.

Jason, H. (2001). *Conflict in Nepal and its impact on children: A discussion document, refugee study center*. Oxford: University of Oxford.

Jnawali, D. et al. (2006). *Education of internally displaced children: Provisions and challenges*. Informally Published Manuscript, Center for Educational Innovation and Development (CERID), Tribhuvan Univer, Kathmandu, Nepal.

Joshi, M., & Mason, T. D. (2011). Peasants, patrons, and parties: The tension between clientelism and democracy in Nepal. *International Studies Quarterly*, 151–157. doi:10.1111/j.1468-2478.2010.00639.x

Judson, R. (1998). Economic growth and investment in education: How allocation matters. *Journal of Economic Growth*, 3(4), 337–359. Retrieved from www.jstor.org/stable/40215992

Kagawa, F. (2005). Emergency education: A critical review of the field. *Comparative Education*, 41(4), 487–503. Retrieved from www.jstor.org/stable/30044557

Kaldor, M., & Luckham, R. (2001). Global transformations and new conflicts. *IDS Bulletin*, 23(2), 48–69. Retrieved from http://onlinelibrary.wiley.com/doi/10.1111/j.1759-5436.2001.mp32002005.x/full

Kaldor, M. (2006). *New and old wars: Organized violence in a global era* (pp. 1–2). Cambridge: Polity Press.

Kantha, P. K. (2010). Maoist-Madhesi dynamics and Nepal's peace process. In M. Lawoti & A. K. Pahari (Eds.), *The Maoist insurgency in Nepal: Revolution in the twenty-first century* (pp. 156–172). London: Routledge.

Karki, A., & Seddon, D. (2003). The People's War in historical context. In A. Karki & D. Seddon (Eds.), *The People's War in Nepal: Left perspectives* (pp. 3–18). New Delhi: Adroit Publishers.

Kattel, M. (2003). Introduction to 'the People's War' and its implications. In A. Karki & D. Seddon (Eds.), *The People's War in Nepal: Left perspectives* (pp. 49–71). New Delhi: Adroit Publishers.

Khaniya, T. R. (2007). *New horizons in education in Nepal* (pp. 117–118). Kathmandu: Kishor Khaniya.

Kindzeka, M. E. (2014, November 25). Camaroon: 130 schools closed due to Boko Haram fears. *Voa News*. Retrieved from www.voanews.com/a/cameroon-130-schools-closed-due-to-boko-haram-fears/2533363.html

Knight, M., & Özerdem, A. (2004). Guns, camps and cash: Disarmament, demobilization and reinsertion of former combatants in transitions from war to peace. *Journal of Peace Research*, 41(4), 499–516. Retrieved from www.jstor.org/stable/4149686

Kohrt, B. (2007). *After war, child soldiers fight a new battle*. Retrieved from http://humanrights.emory.edu/download/ChildSoldier.pdf

Kreisberg, L. (1982). Social conflict theories and conflict resolution. *Peace and Change*, 8(2–3), 3–17. Retrieved from http://onlinelibrary.wiley.com/doi/10.1111/j.1468-0130.1982.tb00644.x/full

Krzyzanowski, M. (2008). Analysing focus group discussions. In R. Wodak & M. Krzyzanowski (Eds.), *Qualitative discourse analysis in the social sciences* (pp. 162–181). London: Macmillan.

Lawoti, M. (2010). *Federal state building: Challenges in the framing the Nepali constitution*. (p. 184). Kathmandu: Bhrikuti Academic Publications.

Lawoti, M., & Pahari, A. K. (2010). Violent conflict and change: Costs and benefits of the Maoist rebellion in Nepal. In M. Lawoti & A. Pahari (Eds.), *The Maoist insurgency in Nepal: Revolution in the twenty first century* (pp. 304–326). New York: Routledge.

Lecomate-Tilouine, M. (2010). Cultural revolution in a Maoist model village. In M. Lawoti & A. Pahari (Eds.), *The Maoist insurgency in Nepal: Revolution in the twenty first century* (pp. 115–132). New York: Routledge.

Machel, G. (1998). *Impact of armed conflict on children*. United Nations. Retrieved from www.un.org/rights/introduc.htm

Mage, J., & D'Mello, B. (2007). The beginning of a new democratic Nepal? *Economic and Political Weekly, 42*(11), 616–620. Retrieved from www.jstor.org/stable/4419354

Manchanda, R. (2006). Making of a 'new Nepal'. *Economic and Political Weekly, 41*(49), 5034–5036. Retrieved from www.jstor.org/stable/4418996

"Maoists Apologize for Baglung Incident," *Kathmandu Post*. (February 20, 2003). In: Watchlist. (2005). *Caught in the middle: Mounting violations against children in Nepal's armed conflict*. Retrieved from http://watchlist.org/caught-in-the-middle-mounting-violations-against-children-in-Nepals-armed-conflict/

Map of Nepal. (2011). Retrieved from www.mapsofworld.com/

McKay, S., & Mazurana, D. E. (2004). *Where are the girls? Girls in fighting forces in Northern Uganda, Sierre Leone and Mozambique: Their lives during and after war*. Montréal, Quebec: Rights & Democracy. Retrieved from https://www1.essex.ac.uk/armedcon/story_id/000478.pdf

Militant siege of Peshawar school ends, 141 killed. (2014, December 16). *Dawn*. Retrieved from https://www.dawn.com/news/1151203

Miller, G., & Dingwall, R. (1997). *Context and method in qualitative research problems with interviewing: Experiences with service providers and clients*. London: Sage Publications Inc.

Mitchell, C. (1981). *The structure of international conflict*. London: Macmillan Press Limited.

Morgan, D., & Krueger, R. (1993). When to use focus groups and why. In D. Morgan (Ed.), *Successful focus groups: Advancing the state of the art* (pp. 3–19). London: Sage Publications Inc.

Moshman, D. (2015). Identity, history, and education in Rwanda: Reflections on the 2014 Nobel Peace Prize. *Child Abuse and Neglect, 44*. Retrieved from https://wp.nyu.edu/e_king/wp-content/uploads/sites/1791/2015/04/ChildAbuseNeglect-2015.pdf

Mottershaw, E. (2008). Economic, social and cultural rights in armed conflict: International Human Rights Law and International Humanitarian Law. *The International Journal of Human Rights, 12*(3).

Mungiu-Pippidi, A. (2010). Twenty years of post communism: The other transition. *Journal of Democracy, 21*(1), 120–127. Project Muse. 2011, September 21. Retrieved from http://muse.jhu.edu/journals/jod/summary/v021/21.1.mungiu-pippidi.html

Muni, S. D. (2004). *Maoist insurgency in Nepal: The challenge and the response* (p. 134). New Delhi: Rupa & Co.

# References

National Anthems. (2007). Retrieved from www.nationalanthems.info/np.htm

The Nepal National Education Planning Commission. (1956). *Education in Nepal.* Kathmandu, Nepal: The Bureau of Publications College of Education Kathmandu. Retrieved from http://www.moe.gov.np/assets/uploads/files/2011_English.pdf

Nepali Congress. (1999). *Nepali congress ko ghoshanapatra.* Kathmandu: Nepali Congress.

Nepali Congress. (2007). *Nepali congress ko ghoshanapatra: Sanvidhansabha nirvachan-2064.* Kathmandu: Nepali Congress.

Nepali, K. (2005, July 29–August 4). Meanwhile the rest of Nepal sees no hope in Kathmandu's continued political paralysis. *Nepali Times.* Retrieved from http://himalaya.socanth.cam.ac.uk/collections/journals/nepalitimes/pdf/Nepali_Times_258.pdf

Nepal Risk Reduction Consortium (NRRC). (2012). Retrieved from www.nrrc.org.np/where-we-work/district-profile.php?d=Sindhupalchok

New, R., & Cochran, M. (2007). Constructionism. In R. New & M. Cochran (Eds.), *Early childhood education: An international encyclopedia* (pp. 149–155). West Port: Pareger. Retrieved from www.praeger.com

Nicolai, S. UNESCO-IIEP. (2009). *Opportunity for change: Education innovation and reform during and after conflict.* Paris: UNESCO-IIEP.

Nussbaum, M. (2007). *The clash within: Democracy, religious violence, and India's future.* Harvard: Belknap Press of Harvard University Press.

OECD. (2001). *Schooling for tomorrow: What schools for the future.* Paris: OECD, Centre for Educational Research and Innovation. Retrieved from http://www.oecd-ilibrary.org/education/what-schools-for-the-future_9789264195004-en

Onta, P. (1996) cited in Velantin, K. (Ed.). (2006). *School for the future: Educational policy and everyday life among urban squatters in Nepal.* Greenwich, CT: Information Age Publishing.

Onta, P. (2000, November 18). Education: Finding a ray of hope. *Economic and Political Weekly, 35*(47).

OSRSG-CAAC. (2009). Retrieved from https://childrenandarmedconflict.un.org/publications/WorkingPaper-1_SixGraveViolationsLegalFoundation.pdf

Page, K. (2003, September 20). *Run and hide: From school to displaced person's center and back to school in Liberia.* Retrieved from http://reliefweb.int/node/134551

Pandey, N. N. (2010). *New Nepal: The fault lines* (p. 164). New Delhi: Sage Publications.

Parker, S., Standing, K., & Pant, B. (2012, September). Caught in the cross fire: Children's right to education during conflict – The case of Nepal 1996–2006. *Children and Society, 27*(5), 372–384.

Pherali, T. J. (2011). Education and conflict in Nepal: Possibilities for reconstruction. *Globalization, Societies and Education, 9*(1). Retrieved from http://www.tandfonline.com/doi/abs/10.1080/14767724.2010.513590?mobileUi=0&journalCode=cgse20

# References

Pherali, T. J. (2015). Education, conflict and development. *Educational Research, 57*(1).

Philip, S. (2004). Curriculum development: Diversity and division in Bosnia and Herzegovina. In S. Tawil & A. Harley (Eds.), *Education, conflict and social cohesion*. Geneva: UNESCO-IBE.

Pigg, S. L. (1992, July). Inventing social categories through place: Social representations and development in Nepal. *Comparative Studies in Society and History, 34*(3), 491–513. Retrieved from https://annastirrdotcom.files.wordpress.com/2013/06/piggnepal1992.pdf

Pradip, N. (2003). The Maoist movement and its impact in Nepal. In A. Karki & D. Seddon (Eds.), *The People's War in Nepal: Left perspectives* (p. 424). New Delhi: Adroit Publishers.

Raeper, W., & Hoftun, M. (1992). *Spring awakening: An account of the 1990 revolution in Nepal*. Nepal: Viking.

Ramsbotham, O., Miall, H., & Woodhouse, T. (2011). Introduction to conflict resolution: Concepts and definitions. In *Contemporary conflict resolution* (3rd ed., pp. 3–34). Cambridge, UK: Polity Press.

Rana, P. S. (1998). The evolution of Nepali nationalism. In D. N. Dhungel & P. S. Rana (Eds.), *Contemporary Nepal* (p. 266). Delhi: Vikas Publishing House.

The Report of the National Education Commission. (1992). *Ministry of Education, Government of Nepal*. Retrieved from http://www.moe.gov.np/assets/uploads/files/2049_English_Summary.pdf

Roberts, S. UNESCO. (2005). *Saving lives, saving minds-education today*. Paris: UNESCO.

Royal Government of Nepal, Ministry of Education and Sports. (2004a). *Mero serofero-class 1*. Bhaktapur: Pathyakram Vikas Kendra.

Royal Government of Nepal, Ministry of Education and Sports. (2004b). *Mero desh-class 5*. Bhaktapur: Pathyakram Vikas Kendra.

Royal Government of Nepal, Ministry of Education and Sports. (2005). *Mero desh-class 4*. Bhaktapur: Pathyakram Vikas Kendra.

Sargent, M. (1994). *The new sociology for Australians*. Retrieved from http://en.wikipedia.org/wiki/Sociology-of-education

Save the Children. (2007). *Rewrite the future*. Retrieved from www.savethechildren.net/rewritethefuture

Save the Children. (2013). *Attacks on education: The impact of conflict and grave violations on children's future*. Retrieved from http://www.savethechildren.org/atf/cf/%7B9def2ebe-10ae-432c-9bd0-df91d2eba74a%7D/ATTACKS_ON_EDUCATION_FINAL.PDF

Save the Children. (2014). *Futures under threat: The impact of the education crisis on Syria's children*. Retrieved from http://www.savethechildren.org/atf/cf/%7B9def2ebe-10ae-432c-9bd0-df91d2eba74a%7D/FUTURES_UNDER_THREAT.PDF

Sears, A. (2008). *A guide to theoretical thinking*. Retrieved from http://en.wikipedia.org/wiki/Conflict_theory

# References

Seddon, D. (1987). *Nepal: A state of poverty* (p. 288). Delhi: Vikas Publishing House.
Shakya, S. (2003). The Maoist movement in Nepal: An analysis from the women. In A. Karki & D. Seddon (Eds.), *The People's War in Nepal: Left perspectives* (p. 494). New Delhi: Adriot Publishers.
Sharda, B. D. (1977). *Status attainment in rural India* (p. 186). Delhi: Ajanta Publications.
Sharma, G. N. (1990). The impact of education during the Rana period in Nepal. *Himalaya, 10*(2), 3–7. Retrieved from http://digitalcommons.macalester.edu/cgi/viewcontent.cgi?article=1255&context=himalaya
Sharma, P. (2007, June 26). *Political transition in Nepal*. Retrieved from www.telegraphnepal.com
Sharma, R., & Khadka, B. (2006). *Impact of armed conflict in education*. Kathmandu, Nepal: Education Journalists Group.
Singer, H. (2012, May 10). *Inaugural speech for SZOP international seminar*. Kathmandu.
Small Arms Survey. (2003). *Small arms survey 2003: Development denied*. Retrieved from http://www.smallarmssurvey.org/publications/by-type/yearbook/small-arms-survey-2003.html
Small Arms Survey. (2015). *Global burden of armed violence 2015: Every body counts*. Retrieved from www.smallarmssurvey.org
Smith, H. L., & Cheung, P. P. L. (1986). Trends in the effects of family background on educational attainment in the Philippines. *American Journal of Sociology, 91*(6), 1387–1408. Retrieved from www.jstor.org/stable/2779801
Smith, T. B. (1981). Nepal's political system in transition. *The World Today, 37*(2), 74–80. Retrieved from www.jstor.org/stable/40395264
Sommers, M., & Buckland, P. (2004). *Parallel worlds, rebuilding the education system in Kosovo* (p. 177). Paris: UNESCO/IIEP.
Srestha, A., & Upreti, M. (Eds.). (2006). *Conflict resolution and governess in Nepal*. Kathmandu: Nepal Foundation for Advanced Studies.
Stalenoi, I. (2014). "The people's war" and Johan Galtung's conflict models. *The Public Administration and Social Policies Review, 1*(12), 32–44. Retrieved from http://revad.uvvg.ro/files/nr12/3.Ionut_Stalenoi.pdf
Stash, S., & Hannum, E. (2001). Who goes to school? Educational stratification by gender, caste, and ethnicity in Nepal. *Comparative Education Review, 45*(3), 354–378.
Tawil, S. (Ed.). (2002). *Curriculum change and social inclusion: Perspectives from the Baltic and Scandinavian countries: Final report of the regional seminar held in Vilnius, Lithuania, 5–8 December 2001* (p. 96). Geneva: UNESCO.
Tawil, S. (2003). *Curriculum change and social cohesion in conflict affected societies*. Geneva: UNESCO-IBE.
Tawil, S., Harley, A., & Braslavsky, C. (Eds.). (2004). *Education, conflict and social cohesion* (p. 433). Geneva: UNESCO-IBE.
Teacher's license test, will it do any good. (2006). Retrieved from www.myrepublica.com/portal/index.php?action=news_details&news_id=32526

## References

10,000 non-Nepali school teachers to be sacked. (2005, November 9). *The Himalayan Times*, 2.

Thapa, M. M., & Koirala, B. N. (2012). *Schools as zones of peace: Nepal's experience.* Report presented in International Seminar on Schools as Zones of Peace, 9–11 May 2012, Hotel Summit, Sanepa, Kathmandu, Nepal.

Theirworld. (2017, February 28). *10 countries where child soldiers are still recruited in armed conflicts.* Retrieved from https://reliefweb.int/report/central-african-republic/10-countries-where-child-soldiers-are-still-recruited-armed

Tilly, C. (2002, Summer). Violence, terror, and politics as usual. *Boston Review.* Retrieved from http://bostonreview.net/archives/BR27.3/tilly.html

Tiwari, V. N. (2010). An assessment of the causes of conflicts in Nepal. In M. Lawoti & A. Pahari (Eds.), *The Maoist insurgency in Nepal: Revolution in the twenty first century* (pp. 241–262). New York: Routledge.

Tumin, M. M. (1985). *Social stratification, the forms and functions of inequality* (2nd ed., p. 166). New Delhi: Prentice Hall of India Pvt. Ltd.

Turin, M. (2005). Language endangerment and linguistic rights in the Himalayas: A case study from Nepal. *Mountain Research and Development*, 25(1), 4–9. Retrieved from www.jstor.org/discover/10.2307/3674361

12 point agreement between Seven Parties and Maoist. (2012, April 24). Retrieved from www.southasiaanalysis.org

UNESCO, EFA Global Monitoring Report. (2011). *The hidden crisis: Armed conflict and education.* Paris: UNESCO.

UNESCO, Towards Universalization of Primary Education in Asia and the Pacific, Country Studies–Nepal. (1984). *The drop out problem in primary education.* Bangkok: UNESCO.

UNESCO. (2010). *Education under attack.* Paris: UNESCO. Retrieved from http://unesdoc.unesco.org/images/0018/001868/186809e.pdf

UNESCO. (2011). *The hidden crisis: Armed conflict and education (Summary).* Education for All Monitoring Report (p. 6). Retrieved from http://unesdoc.unesco.org/images/0019/001911/191186e.pdf

UNESCO. (2013, July). Children still battling to go to school. Education for All. *Policy Paper 10.* Retrieved from http://unesdoc.unesco.org/images/0022/002216/221668E.pdf

UNHCR. (2005). Technology of warfare and children. *Refugees*, 2(139).

UNICEF. (2005a). *Quality education for all in Kosovo.* New York: UNICEF.

UNICEF. (2005b). *The state of the world's children report.* New York: UNICEF.

UNICEF. (2012). *Schools as zones of peace.* Retrieved from https://www.unicef.org/infobycountry/nepal_65410.html

UNICEF. (2014). *Annual report on Nepal.* Retrieved from https://www.unicef.org/about/annualreport/files/Nepal_Annual_Report_2014.pdf

United Nations. (1989). *Convention on the rights of the child.* Retrieved from www.un.org/pubs/cyberschoolbus/treaties/child.asp

United Nations. (2012). *Comprehensive peace agreement of Nepal* [Translated]. Retrieved From www.un.org.np/node/10498

# References

United Nations Human Rights Office of the High Commissioner. (2015). Retrieved from http://www.ohchr.org/EN/ProfessionalInterest/Pages/InternationalCriminalCourt.aspx

Upreti, B. C. (2008). *Maoists in Nepal: From insurgency to political mainstream*. Delhi: Kalpaz Publications.

Upreti, B. R. (2004). *The price of neglect: Conflict to Maoist insurgency in the Himalayan kingdom* (p. 446). Kathmandu: Bhrikuti Academic Publications.

Varma, A. S. (2005). *Nepal ka jan yudh* (pp. 1–16). New Delhi: Udbhavana Pustika.

Vaux, T., Smith, A., & Subba, S. (2003, January 31). *Education for all – Nepal, Review from a conflict perspective, international alert*. Retrieved from www.international-alert.org/resources/publications/education-all-%E2%80%93-Nepal

Watchlist. (2005). *Caught in the middle: Mounting violations against children in Nepal's armed conflict*. Retrieved from https://www1.essex.ac.uk/armedcon/story_id/000249.pdf

van Wessel, M., & van Hirtum, R. (2011). Schools as tactical targets in conflict: What the case of Nepal can teach us. Retrieved from http://www.journals.uchicago.edu/doi/abs/10.1086/667530

Watchlist. (2005). *Caught in the middle: Mounting violations against children in Nepal's armed conflict*. Retrieved from http://watchlist.org/caught-in-the-middle-mounting-violations-against-children-in-Nepals-armed-conflict/

Whelpton, J. (1993). The general elections of May, 1991. In M. Hutt (Ed.), *Nepal in nineties* (pp. 48–81). New Delhi: Oxford University Press.

Whelpton, J. (2005). *A history of Nepal* (1st ed., p. 296). Cambridge: Cambridge University Press.

The World Bank. (2013). *World development indicators*. Washington, DC: The World Bank. Retrieved from http://databank.worldbank.org/data/download/WDI-2013-ebook.pdf

Xaykaothao, D. (2006, September 1). *Women, children feel effects of Nepal's insurgency*. Retrieved from www.internationalreportingproject.org

Yusufzai, A. (2011, June 26). Schools rise from the rubble. *IPS News*. Retrieved from http://ipsnews.net/news.asp?idnews=56234

# Appendix

Schools as Zones of Peace
Kathmandu Guiding Principles (FINAL DRAFT)
Issued by the Representatives attending the International Seminar on Schools as Zones of Peace
May 2012, Kathmandu, Nepal

## Introduction

Of the estimated 67 million children out of school worldwide as many as 25 million live in countries affected by conflict. Education is an important intervention in emergencies, as it can provide physical, psychosocial and cognitive protection to children. All children have a right to quality education in all situations and at all times, including emergencies. Lack of information and education plays a key role in involving population in conflicts.

Following an initiative by the Ministry of Education/Government of Nepal, Ministry of Foreign Affairs/Government of Norway, UNICEF and Save the Children organized an International Seminar on Schools as Zones of Peace (SZOP) in Kathmandu from 9 to 11 May 2012.

Representatives from India, Ivory Coast, Liberia, Nepal, Norway and South Sudan participated. The seminar included High level officials, representing the Governments, Development Partner Groups, International/Non-Government Organizations, Civil Society Organizations, and community stakeholders including students, teachers, parents and media academics.

The seminar was held in Kathmandu in recognition of the valuable experience that Nepal has gained in its efforts to promote and protect schools in a conflict and post conflict environment to ensure they are free from violence, discrimination and political activities through the Schools as Zones of Peace education concept. The seminar provided an opportunity for sharing experiences, based on the lessons learnt in different conflict contexts.

## Common understanding on SZOP

- The seminar participants endorsed Schools as Zones of Peace as an important concept and approach to promoting safe and secure learning and teaching environments.
- Guiding principles should be to ensure that the home, school and community are all connected for peace.
- There is a need to respect diversity, identity and equity as these are often sources of conflict.
- Neutrality in dealing with all stakeholders is important. Respect of children's voices equally so.
- There is critical work to be done on curriculum development.
- Plans must be locally adaptable and flexible to conflict situations.
- The process of developing a Code of Conduct needs to be followed.
- Schools should under no pretext be closed to fulfill the demands of adult groups
- Governance/law and order must not be compromised.
- Engaging non-state actors must be better understood.
- The participants recognized that fulfilling the vision of Schools as Zones of Peace requires access to human and financial resources, and called for cooperation between national and international development partners in making necessary resources available.

## Common Understanding of Roles

- The seminar recognized the importance of mobilizing and empowering **children** as promoters of peace, including specific efforts to establish Schools as Zones of Peace.
- The participants recognized the pivotal role of **teachers** as agents of change and their professional organizations for securing uninterrupted services in schools, especially during conflict situations.
- The seminar participants recognized and endorsed that **parents** can play a major part in creating safe and enabling environments in and around schools.

*Appendix* 131

- Participants expressed the overriding and pivotal role of **political parties** in contributing to a safe and uninterrupted learning environment where students and teachers can pursue their work without intimidation and fear.
- Participants agreed that the **media** can play a significant role in building awareness and accountability about the impact of conflict on education, inform the stakeholders about the measures that can be taken to protect and uphold the right to education in all circumstances and hold responsible parties accountable for ensuring school safety and continued access.
- The participants agreed that **academia** has a critical role to play in terms of generating ideas changing the perception of politicians and the public at large, as well as in contributing to building a culture of peace through development of syllabus and teacher training.
- The participants recognized the importance of **Civil Society** in mobilizing communities and drawing attention of the governments at the national and international levels for the protection and promotion of education in conflict situations, and work as advocates for promoting the right to education for all children, including children living in conflict affected areas
- Participants acknowledged that **Non-Governmental Organizations** can play an important role in building capacity for the continuation of education in conflict affected areas through networking at the local level and help provide targeted services in close cooperation with national education authorities.
- The participants of the seminar declared that **Governments** has a responsibility to create enabling environment and make students, teachers and school community feel safe. The participants also reiterated that Governments should give priority to maintaining law and order to sustain peace and secure safe learning environments in schools, upholding the principle of Schools as Zones of Peace.
- The participants agreed that the **Education Ministries** need to work more closely with the **International development partners** for mobilizing resources and institutionalizing service delivery mechanisms to ensure uninterrupted school functioning, and create environments conducive for promoting peace and harmony in difficult circumstances.
- It is critical to involve **state/national authority**, build unity among the different state entities, teachers, children, parents and youth.

## Commitments

- Create common understanding of what the SZOP concept is and how it benefits all.
- Drafting/articulating a SZOP framework and sharing it widely.
- Draft country generic guidelines on how to implement SZOP.
- Organize and be part of other movements, such as the Global Coalition to Protect Education from Attack (GCPEA).
- Continue to share experiences with other countries with similar problems.

## Follow-up Actions

- Share and engage key stakeholders in respective countries on the outcome of the international seminar and concept of SZOP.
- Invite relevant stakeholders to a common platform for discussing SZOP.
- Documenting the experience from this seminar.
- To have follow up meetings on a national basis.
- Have press meets to share with wider public.

# Index

Page numbers in italic indicate a figure and page numbers in bold indicate a table on the corresponding page.

Acharya, U. D. 52
Al Abdullah, Rania 16–17
All Nepal National Independent Student's Union (ANNISU) 42
All Nepal Revolutionary Coordination Committee (ML) 32
All-round National Education Commission 49–50
Anglo-Nepalese war, 1814-16 27
Aryal, Gokharan 79

Baidya, Mohan 33
Balhit Secondary School 80
*bandhs* 96–97
Baraily, Balman 80–81
Basic and Primary Education Programme (BPEP) 52, 56
Basnet, Narjit 79, 80, 95
Bhairab Nath Lower Secondary School 80
Bhandari, Madan 35–36
Bhattarai, Baburam 33, 36–37, 63, 89, 100
Bhattarai, Hari Prasad 80
Bhattarai, K. P. 35
Bidya Mandir Higher Secondary School 85
Birendra, King 31, 44, 51
Bista, M. 60
Biswokarma, Santosh 77
Blin, A. 9
Brabant, J. M. V. 99

*Buniyadi Siksha* 47
bureaucracy 41–42

Caddell, Martha 49, 51, 60, 64, 65
caste 60–61, 68–69
*Chamkelo Taro, Itihasik Dastaveze* 89
children: involved in armed conflict 11–12, 15–17, 75–76, **82–83**, 88–92, 93–95; living in war zones 86, **86–87**; of martyrs 105; out-of-school 88–92; recruitment by the Maoist movement 93–95; technological advancements and 17; trafficking of 79
*Child Workers in Nepal* 86
Chisapani Higher Secondary School 80
community-based Education Information Management System (C-EMIS) 55
Community Study and Welfare Centre (CSWC) 74
Comprehensive Peace Agreement of 2006 78, 98, 100
conflict: academic attention on 1–4, *2*; children in armed 11–12, 15–17, 75–76, **82–83**, 88–92, 93–95; classroom implications of 21–22; containment of 7, 7–8; countries affected with 114–115; from the education perspective 8–11; education quality and 23;

escalation and de-escalation of 4, 4–8, 7; financial implications of 20–21; Galtung's model of 2, 2, 2–4; gender and 22–23; hourglass model of 6–7; Marxist perspective on 12–15; relative deprivation theory 5–6; social 3; transformation 7, 7–8; understanding 1–4, 2
conflict analysis model 2
*confligere* 1
Conteh-Morgan, E. 5–6
contradiction 2, 2
CPN (Communist Party of Nepal) 25–26; beginning of the People's War and 38–39; demand for elected Constituent Assembly 30; education policies 53–55, 59; elections, 1991 35–36; end of the People's War and 98–100; formation of 28; general elections of 1999 and 43–44; leadership and division 33; 1994 elections and making of 36–37; preparing the ground for the People's War 37–38; recruitment of child soldiers 94–95
CPN-UML (United Marxist Lennist) 35–36
culture of violence 3
Curriculum, Textbooks and Supervision Development Centre (CTSDC) 50

Darbar High School 46
de-escalation and escalation of conflict 4, 4–8, 7
Delhi Compromise 29
democracy, pluralistic 99–100
democratic government in Nepal 29–30; movement of 1990 34–35
Devkota Primary School 81

Early Childhood Development (ECD) 56–57
economic zones of Nepal 24
education: classroom implications of conflict and 21–22; conflict and public 15–17; conflict from the perspective of 8–11; engaging with theoretical framework on conflict and 12–15; quality and conflict 23; teachers 17–20, 42–43, 64; vocational 50
education in Nepal: administrative structure of 55–56; All-round National Education Commission 49–50; attacks on schools and 84–86; caste and 60–61, 68–69; changes since 2007 100; for the classes and not for the masses 67–69, 68; closure of schools and 96–97; early childhood development 56–57; exclusion and spade work for the People's War 58–63; financial implications of conflict and 20–21; forbidden under the Rana regime 27; 40-point charter of demands 102–103; framework for schools as zones of peace and 105; general administrative system 55–56; hope in new era of 105–109; interim constitution, 2007, and 103–104; letter to revise curriculum and content, 2007 110–113; migration and 19–20; Ministry of Education and Sports/Ministry of Education 56–57; in modern times 46–48; National Curriculum Framework (NCF) 57–58; National Primary Schools 49; *Nepal Sarkar* 100–101, **101–102**; New Education System Plan (NESP) 50–51; new integrated school system after 2007 104; 1951–1960 48–49; 1960–1970 49–50; overcrowded classrooms and 92; during the People's War 54–55; primary and secondary education 57, 66; in private schools 62, 65–66, 85; reality or myth of free 69–70, 70; religious 45; Sanskrit and 65–66; scholarship for children of martyrs 105; school leaving certificate (SLC) 51; schools as strategic places and 88, 96–97; state of, 1970-1980 50–52; state of, 1980-1990 52; state of, 1990-2007 52–54; students and teachers as supporters and sufferers in 74–84, **77, 81, 82–83**;

Index    135

suspension of funds for 93; teachers in 70–71, 104; textbooks 51, 71–73, 72, **101–102**, 105; wider world view and enhanced aspirations as a result of 39–40
Education Journalists' Group of Nepal 64, 80, 81
elite peacemaking 7, 7–8
escalation and de-escalation of conflict 4, 4–8, 7
ethnic federalism 98
ethnic groups of Nepal 24–25, 98, 109
exclusion, sociopolitical 40–41; People's War, education and 58–63

"Felicity's Condition" 81
financial implications of conflict 20–21
40-point charter of demands 102–103
functionalism 14

Galtung, Johan 2, 2, 2–4
Gandak Bureau of Maoists 80
Gandhi, Indira 31
gender: conflict and 22–23; People's War and 60; sexual violence and 15–16, 78–79; sociopolitical exclusion and injustice related to 40–41; in the war zone 95–96
general administrative system, education 55–56
Geneva Conventions 76, 84
Global Burden of Armed Violence report 10–11
gross national income (GNI), Nepal 25
Gurung, Jamadar Sripati 27
Gurung, Yam Bahadur 86
Gyanendra, King 28, 44, 72, 73

hegemony: national anthem and 73; textbooks and 71–73, 72
Hoftun, M. 32
hourglass model of conflict 6–7
Human Rights Watch 95
human trafficking 79

Iglic, H. 99
India: education spending in 9; independence 27–28; Maoists in 13; National Congress and Indira Gandhi 31; Naxal movement in 32–33; shared cultural history between Nepal and 25; Sugauli treaty with Nepal 27; support for constitutional monarchy in Nepal 28–29
Informal Service Sector Centre (INSEC) 76, 86
injustice 40–41
Interim Constitution 103–104
International Criminal Court (ICC) 75, 76
inter-state conflict 6
intra-state war 6
Iritar Secondary School 86
Isajiw, W. W. 99

*Jana Andolan* 65
Janak Printing Press 62
Jhapa guerrilla movement *see* People's War, the
Johnson, Chalmers 14

K. C., Tilak 81
Kalika School 80
*Kantipur* 85
Karki, A. 27
*karmkand* 45
Karnali Higher Secondary School 80
*Kathmandu Post* 75
Katuwal, Chakra Bahadur 82
Khasas 26
Koirala, Dak Mani 80
Koirala, Durga Prasad 80
Koirala, Girija Prasad 35–36, 62, 103, 109
Koirala, M. P. 28, 29–30
Kuhibhir Secondary School 82
Kumari, Sita 86

Lama, Nirmal 33, 36
legislative elections: first democratic 29–30; mid-term, 1994 36; 1999 43–44; 1991 35–36
letter to revise curriculum and content, 2007 110–113
light-weight weapons 17

Mahat, Som Bhadur 82
Mahendra, King 29–31, 48
Mahendra Sanskrit University 66
Manchanda, R. 95

Maoist movement 13, 25, 32–33; child soldiers and 77–78; education policies 53–55, 81–84; end of the People's War and 98–100; parallel governments and 92–93; People's Court and 41–42; recruitment of children 93–95; resistance to Sanskrit 66; teachers and 42–43; women and 95–96; *see also* CPN (Communist Party of Nepal); People's War, the
Mao Tse-Tung 32–33
Marxism: Naxal movement and 32–33; perspective on conflict 12–15
Mazumdar, Charu 32
media and awareness of common issues 39
mid-term elections, 1994 36
migration 19–20, 78
Millennium Development Goals (MDGs) 10
Ministry of Education and Sports 56–57
Mitchell, Chris 2
mobility inertia 45–46
Modern Indian School 85
Mukti Sena 28
multi-party legislative elections, 1991 35–36
*Muluki Ain* 61

national anthem 73, 102
National Centre for Educational Development (NCED) 104
National Curriculum Framework (NCF) 57–58
National Education Commission 52–53
National Framework for Capacity Development 109
National Legal Code 61
National Plan of Action 57
National Primary Schools 49
Naxal movement, India 32–33
Nepal 24; ban on political parties in 30–32; bureaucracy and slow decision-making processes in 41–42; caste in 60–61; democracy movement of 1990 in 34–35; as democratic republic 99; economic zones 24; education in (*see* education in Nepal); emergence of modern 26–29; ethnic groups of 24–25, 98, 109; expansion of media and awareness of common issues in 39; first elected democratic government in 29–30; gross national income (GNI) 25; influence of the Naxal movement in India on 32–33; interim constitution, 2007 103–104; letter to revise curriculum and content, 2007 110–113; literacy rate 25; mid-term elections, 1994 36; multi-party legislative elections, 1991 35–36; national anthem 73, 102; political history of 25–26; sociocultural context of 24–26; sociocultural exclusion and injustice in 40–41; third general elections, 1999 43–44; wider world view and enhanced aspirations of people in 39–40
Nepali Congress Party 28–30; elections, 1991 35–36
Nepali Democratic Congress 28
Nepal Janbadi Morcha 33
Nepal National Education Planning Commission 49
*Nepal Sarkar* 100–101, **101–102**
New Education System Plan (NESP) 50–51
Nicolai, S. 64
*Niji Srot* teachers 71

out-of-school children 88–92
overcrowded classrooms 92

Panchayat system 31–32, 34–35, 39, 65–66, 73, 99
Panini Sanskrit High School 66
parallel governments 92–93
Parishad, Praja 27
Parsons, Talcott 14
*pathsaalas* 51, 65
peacebuilding 2, 2, 7, 7–8
People's Court 41–42, 61
People's Front 33

People's Liberation Army (PLA) 38, 75, 77–78, 82; child soldiers in 86–87, 89–92; women and 95–96
People's War, the 32; attacks on schools during 84–86; beginning of 38–39; education, exclusion and spade work for 58–63; education during 54–55; end of 98; parallel government during 92–93; preparing the ground for 37–38; resistance to Sanskrit and 65–66; scholarships for children of martyrs in 105; schools as strategic places in 88; students and teachers as supporters and sufferers in 74–84, 77, 81, 82–83; suspension of funds for education 93; teachers and 42–43, 64; women in the war zone during 95–96
Peshawar military school, Pakistan 1
Pherali, Tejendra J. 83
political parties, ban on 30–32
Prachanda (Pushpa Kamal Dahal) 33, 36, 98, 103
Prasikshan, Sainya 89
primary and secondary education 49, 57, 66
Primary Education Project 52
private schools 62, 65–66, 85
public schooling *see* education

quality of education 23

Radio Nepal 31
Rana, Dev Shumsher 47
Rana, Jung Bahadur 27, 46
Rana, Padma Shamsher 29
Rana rulers 27–29
Rastriya Panchayat 31–32
relative deprivation theory 5–6
religious education 45
right to education 15
Roberts, Beverly 15

Sadbhavana Party 40
Samyukta Rastriya Janaandolan (United National People's Movement) 35
Sandhu Secondary School 83

Sanskrit 65–66
Sanyal, Kanu 32
Save the Children 18–19, 55
schooling *see* education
school leaving certificate (SLC) 51
School Sector Reform Plan of 2009 105
Sears 6
Secondary Education Development Project 52
Seddon, D. 27
Sen, Mukund 26
sexual violence 15–16, 78–79
Shah, Dravya 26
Shah, Prithvi Narayan, King 25, 26–27
Shamsher, Mohan 29
Sharma 99
*Shishu Kaksha* 56
Shree Sharada High Secondary School 88
Shrestha, Krishna Gopal 81–82
Shrestha, Marich Man Singh 32, 34
Shrestha, Pushpa Lal 28
Siddhi Ganesh Secondary School 80
Singh, Mohan Bikram 33, 36
Singh, Ram Raja Prasad 33
Singh, Sona 86
Siwakoti, Udhav 81
Small Arms Survey 10
SMCs (school management committees): financial management by 52; integrated school system role of 104; new provisions for 103; *Niji Srot* teachers and 71; restructuring of 100; teacher management role 104
social conflict 3
social constructivism 5
sociocultural context of Nepal 24–26
State of the World's Children Report 14
St. Joseph's School 85
strikes 96–97
structural violence 2, 2
Subedi, Harsa 79
Sugauli treaty 27

Tawil, S. 109
teachers: as backbone of the Maoist movement 42–43; conflict and 17–20; management of 70–71; murder of 64; overcrowded classrooms and 92; recruitment after 2007 104; and students as supporters and sufferers in Nepal's education system 74–84, 77, 81, **82–83**
technological advancements and child soldiers 17
textbooks 51, 71–73, 72; 40-point charter of demands and 102–103; hegemony and 69–70, **70**; language issue in 105; letter to revise curriculum and content, 2007 110–113; photographs in new 103; since 2007 **101–102**
Tilly, Charles 8
trafficking, human 79
Treason Act of 1961 31
Tribhuvan, King 28–29
Tumin, M. M. 106

UNESCO 84
UNICEF 14, 17, 25
United Front of Nepali 34–35
United Left Front 34–35

United Nations: Convention on the Rights of the Child 11, 16, 75, 76; Education for All 10; Millennium Development Goals (MDGs) 11–12
United People's Front of Nepal (UPFN) 35–36; beginning of the People's War and 38–39; preparing the ground for the People's War 37–38

Vaidya, Niranjan Govind 36
Vaux, T. 55
Vigyan, Sainya Akhil 89
vocational education 50

Watchlist report **77**
women and girls: gender issues in conflict and 22–23; living in the war zone 95–96; sexual violence against 15–16, 78–79
Wood, Hugh 27, 45–46
Wright, Quincy 2

Yaksh Mall 26
Yashma Secondary School 82
Yogi, Dalkaji 81
Yousafzai, Malala 15

zones of peace, schools as 105